THE CONTAINER GARDEN BLUEPRINT

EASY STEPS TO LUSH, SMALL-SPACE GARDENING

BY AMELIA GROVE

TABLE OF CONTENTS

For DEV, who could grow anything, anywhere.

WELCOME!

Not long ago, I found myself staring at a small pot of wilting basil on my kitchen windowsill. It was my first attempt at container gardening. I had imagined lush greenery sprouting with little effort. But reality was different. The leaves were droopy, and I was clueless. Yet, at that moment of frustration, I felt a spark of determination. I decided to learn from my mistakes and find out what makes plants thrive in small spaces. That journey led me to more than just a flourishing herb garden. It led me to a passion for container gardening that I am excited to share with you.

This book is about making container gardening accessible and fun for beginners like you. My goal is to break down complex gardening ideas into simple steps. I want to empower you with the knowledge you need to create your own small-space oasis. Whether you have a tiny balcony or just a kitchen counter, you can grow something beautiful and rewarding.

Container gardening is perfect for those with limited space. It offers flexibility and creativity and lets you bring nature to urban environments. You can move your plants to find the best sunlight, experiment with colors and textures, and even grow your own herbs and vegetables. The possibilities are endless, and they fit right into your lifestyle.

Many beginners worry that gardening is too hard or that they lack a green thumb. But I promise, success is within your reach. We'll tackle common fears and misconceptions together. You'll see that each step is simple and manageable. With this book, you'll have the support you need to start with confidence.

Gardening is a personal journey. It should reflect your style and fit your space. This book will guide you in choosing plants and containers that match your preferences. You'll learn how to create a garden that feels uniquely yours.

Planning is critical to gardening success. That's why we've included seasonal planting guides. These will help you stay engaged and productive throughout the year. You'll know exactly what to plant and when, ensuring your garden thrives in every season.

What sets this book apart is its unique blend of practical strategies and inspiration. It's not just a guide; it's a companion on your gardening journey. We're also building a sense of community among readers, fostering a network of shared knowledge and support.

Container gardening offers more than just visual beauty. It provides mental and emotional benefits. We've integrated mindfulness exercises and stress-relief techniques. As you garden, you'll find peace and joy in nurturing life.

As you hold this book, I invite you to take the first step on your gardening journey. With each page, you'll discover new techniques and insights. You'll grow in confidence and skill. Together, we'll create a lush, small-space oasis that brings joy to your life. Welcome to the world of container gardening. It's a journey filled with growth and discovery, and I am thrilled to be your guide.

CHAPTER 1:
LAYING THE FOUNDATION FOR SUCCESS

Every thriving garden begins with a strong foundation, and container gardening is no different. If you've ever felt frustrated by droopy plants, stubborn soil, or limited space, you're not alone. Like many first-time gardeners, my journey began with a few pots, big dreams, and plenty of mistakes. But through trial, error, and a lot of learning, I discovered the keys to creating lush, thriving gardens, even in the tiniest spaces. This chapter is all about setting you up for success, covering everything you need to know to get started with container gardening.

We'll begin by exploring the basics of container gardening, breaking down why it's such a versatile and accessible way to grow plants. From herbs on a windowsill to flowers on a balcony, you'll discover that your garden's size is limited only by your imagination. Next, we'll dive into the all-important task of **choosing the right containers**—balancing size, material, and style to create the perfect home for your plants. You'll learn that the right pot isn't just functional—it can elevate the look and feel of your entire garden.

Of course, no garden can flourish without the right soil. We'll cover how to select and amend **potting mixes** that provide the nutrients, aeration, and drainage your plants need. Speaking of drainage, we'll also explore techniques to prevent waterlogging and keep your plants' roots healthy and happy. With practical tips and personal anecdotes, you'll feel confident tackling this often-overlooked aspect of container gardening.

Tools are another key to success. From trowels to pruners, we'll highlight the **essential gardening tools** that make container gardening efficient and enjoyable. You'll also learn how to care for and even upcycle tools, ensuring your gardening kit lasts for years. Finally, we'll bring it all together with a section on **space planning**, helping you map out your small garden for maximum impact. Whether you're working with a tiny balcony, a sunny patio, or just a few windowsills, we'll show you how to make every inch count.

By the end of this chapter, you'll have the knowledge and confidence to lay a solid foundation for your container garden. Whether you're a total beginner or just looking to refine your skills, this is where your gardening journey truly begins.

1.1 UNDERSTANDING CONTAINER GARDENING: A BEGINNER'S GUIDE

Container gardening is more than just placing a plant in a pot. It's about creating a little ecosystem that thrives on its own, even in the smallest spaces. Think of it as gardening without the need for a sprawling backyard. It's perfect for apartments or homes with limited outdoor areas. This method uses containers like pots, buckets, or even upcycled items to grow plants that might otherwise be impossible in a traditional garden setting. The beauty of container gardening lies in its versatility and adaptability to urban environments. You can move pots around to catch the best sunlight or even bring them indoors when the weather turns harsh.

The variety of plants you can grow in containers is astounding. Your options are vast, from luscious herbs like basil and mint to colorful flowers and even vegetables like tomatoes and peppers. You can enjoy a fragrant herb garden on your kitchen windowsill or a collection of vibrant flowers on your balcony. Plus, you can switch it up throughout the year, growing seasonally appropriate plants to keep your garden fresh and exciting. No matter the season, there's something you can cultivate.

It's normal to feel a bit overwhelmed at the start, but let me reassure you—anyone can succeed with container gardening. Begin with easy-start plants that are forgiving and require minimal fuss. If you're worried about not having a green thumb, know that many have felt the same way and still created incredible container gardens. A common myth is that you need a lot of space or fancy equipment to begin. This isn't true. You can turn even the smallest corner into a thriving green space with a few pots and the right plants.

Setting realistic expectations is key. Container gardening does require some time and effort, but it's rewarding. You'll need to water your plants regularly, keep an eye out for pests, and do a bit of pruning now and then. Yet, these tasks aren't chores; they're opportunities to connect with nature and witness growth firsthand. Challenges may arise, like dealing with pests or unexpected weather changes, but these are part of the learning process. Each challenge is an opportunity to learn and strengthen your gardening skills.

Here are 4 quick-start tips for your container garden:
- Choose beginner-friendly plants for your first attempt.
- Pick a sunny spot where your plants will get at least 6 hours of light daily.

- Use a good potting mix, not garden soil, for better drainage.
- Remember to water only when the top inch of soil is dry to avoid overwatering.

Try some of these 10 beginner-friendly plants:

1. **Pothos (Devil's Ivy)**
   - **Why it's great:** Nearly indestructible, thrives in a variety of light conditions, and offers trailing, lush greenery.
   - **Tips:** Use a hanging pot or let it cascade from a shelf. Water when the top inch of soil is dry.
2. **Snake Plant (Sansevieria)**
   - **Why it's great:** Hardy and drought-tolerant, this plant thrives on neglect and purifies the air.
   - **Tips:** Use a deep container with well-draining soil. Water sparingly, allowing the soil to dry completely between waterings.
3. **Spider Plant**
   - **Why it's great:** Adapts well to most environments and produces "babies" that can be propagated easily.
   - **Tips:** Hang in a basket or place on a shelf. Keep soil slightly moist but not soggy.
4. **Succulents (Echeveria, Haworthia, etc.)**
   - **Why it's great:** Low-maintenance and thrives in small containers with minimal watering.
   - **Tips:** Use shallow pots with cactus soil and provide plenty of bright, indirect light.
5. **Zebra Plant (Aphelandra squarrosa)**
   - **Why it's great:** Striking striped foliage adds visual interest to small spaces.
   - **Tips:** Keep in bright, indirect light and water consistently to maintain humidity.

6. **Peace Lily**
   - **Why it's great:** Elegant, air-purifying plant that thrives in low light and signals its watering needs by drooping.
   - **Tips:** Use a medium-sized pot with rich soil. Water when the leaves start to droop slightly.
7. **Calathea (Prayer Plant)**
   - **Why it's great:** Vibrant, patterned leaves fold up at night, making it a captivating addition to your space.
   - **Tips:** Keep in a well-draining pot with high humidity and water regularly to keep the soil moist.
8. **Dracaena Marginata (Dragon Tree)**
   - **Why it's great:** Tall, slender, and drought-tolerant, it's ideal for creating height in small spaces.
   - **Tips:** Use a pot with good drainage and water when the topsoil feels dry.
9. **Boston Fern**
   - **Why it's great:** Lush, feathery foliage that adds a tropical vibe to any room or balcony.
   - **Tips:** Use a hanging basket or shallow pot with well-draining soil. Mist regularly to maintain humidity.
10. **Lucky Bamboo (Dracaena sanderiana)**
   - **Why it's great:** Symbolizes good fortune and requires minimal care, thriving in water or soil.
   - **Tips:** Grow in a small vase with water and pebbles, ensuring the water level is consistent.

These plants are resilient and beautiful, which makes them a great choice for your new container garden!

1.2 CHOOSING THE RIGHT CONTAINERS:
SIZE, SHAPE, AND MATERIAL

Finding the perfect container is like picking the right shoes for your outfit. It's not just about looks; it's about function and fit. The relationship between the size of your plant and its container is crucial. If you squeeze a large plant into a tiny pot, it's like wearing shoes a size too small—uncomfortable and restrictive. Conversely, placing a small plant in a giant pot can lead to waterlogging, as the soil retains too much moisture. You want to choose a pot that allows enough room for roots to spread but isn't overwhelmingly large. Container shape can also affect plant growth. Tall, narrow pots can lead to top-heavy plants, while wide, shallow pots may suit plants with spreading roots, like succulents. Material choice plays a significant role in how your plants fare. Each material comes with its own set of pros and cons. Terracotta pots, for example, are porous and allow soil to breathe, which can help prevent root rot. However, they can dry out quickly and crack in cold weather. Plastic pots are lightweight and retain moisture well, but they can leach chemicals and may not withstand harsh sunlight over time. Metal containers are durable and weatherproof, they can heat up and potentially burn roots. Wood offers natural insulation but requires maintenance to avoid rot. Understanding these nuances helps you select containers that enhance plant health and fit your environment.

Beyond the technical aspects, the aesthetics of your containers matter, too. Your choice of pots can complement your home decor, creating a seamless transition from indoor to outdoor spaces. Whether you prefer sleek, modern designs or rustic, earthy tones, you can match your style with the proper containers. Consider placing pots at varying heights to add visual interest and make your small garden look dynamic. Remember, the placement of your containers will also affect your plants. Place them where they receive adequate light and are protected from harsh weather.

Sustainability in gardening is becoming increasingly important, and your choice of containers can reflect that. Upcycled and DIY projects offer eco-friendly and cost-effective solutions. Transform old buckets, tins, or even tires into unique planters that add character while reducing waste. Biodegradable materials such as coconut coir or recycled paper pots are also great options. They support plant growth and break down naturally, contributing to a more sustainable gardening practice.

Choosing the right container is the first step toward a thriving garden. It sets the stage for your plants to grow healthy and strong. Remember to consider both the practical and aesthetic aspects, and always choose sustainable options when possible. Your choices here will have a lasting impact on your gardening success.

1.3 THE IMPORTANCE OF SOIL: SELECTING THE PERFECT POTTING MIX

When it comes to container gardening, soil is the unsung hero. It might seem like the least glamorous part of gardening, but it's the foundation upon which your plants thrive. Soil isn't just dirt; it's a living, breathing ecosystem that provides nutrients, retains moisture, and supports plant roots. Choosing the right soil is crucial because it directly impacts plant health. A good potting mix will supply nutrients consistently, allowing plants to absorb what they need to grow strong and vibrant. It will also maintain its structure, providing aeration that lets roots breathe and allows water to infiltrate and drain properly.

Many beginner gardeners think they can simply scoop up some garden soil and plop it into a pot. If this is you, let me stop you right there. Garden soil is too dense for containers. It compacts easily, leading to poor drainage and suffocated roots. A quality potting mix is specially formulated for containers, offering the lightness and fluffiness that garden soil lacks. Typically, a potting mix contains elements like peat moss, compost, or coir, which help retain moisture without becoming waterlogged. It might also include bark or sand for drainage and perlite or vermiculite to keep the soil airy and loose. This combination ensures your plants have the best environment to spread their roots and access the nutrients they crave.

Now, every plant is unique, and sometimes your potting mix might need a little extra something. This is where soil amendments come into play. If your mix drains too quickly, adding perlite or vermiculite can help improve moisture retention. These lightweight, volcanic minerals increase drainage while keeping the soil airy. On the other hand, if your plants seem to lack vigor, incorporating organic matter like compost can boost their nutrient intake. Organic matter enriches the soil, providing essential nutrients and enhancing microbial activity, which is vital for healthy plant growth. It's like giving your plants a nutrient-packed smoothie!

Of course, it's not all smooth sailing. Soil compaction is a common issue in container gardening. When soil particles are pressed together, they reduce the space available for air and water, stunting root growth. Regularly checking your soil and gently loosening it with a fork can prevent this. Also, watch for nutrient deficiencies, which lead to yellowing leaves or stunted growth. These signs might indicate a need for fertilization or a change in the potting mix. Whether it's a shot of liquid fertilizer or a slow-release option, giving your plants the nutrients they need is vital for overcoming these hurdles.

Understanding your soil and how to amend it is a game-changer in container gardening. It's a step that might seem small, but it has a significant impact on the health and vitality of your plants. With the right potting mix and amendments, your container garden will not only survive but thrive, blooming beautifully and producing abundant harvests. Your plants will thank you with vibrant flowers and lush foliage.

1.4 MASTERING DRAINAGE:
TECHNIQUES FOR HEALTHY PLANT ROOTS

Imagine you've just planted your favorite herb in a beautiful pot, and you're eagerly awaiting that first sign of growth. But weeks pass, and the plant looks weak and unhappy instead of thriving. This scenario often traces back to one culprit: poor drainage. Proper drainage is like the unsung hero of container gardening; it's the difference between a flourishing plant and one that struggles to survive. Without it, water accumulates, leading to root rot—a condition where roots are deprived of oxygen and begin to decay. This can be devastating for your plants, as healthy roots are vital for absorbing water and nutrients. Signs of overwatering and poor drainage include yellowing leaves, wilting despite moist soil, and a musty smell from the pot. Recognizing these red flags early can save your plants from an untimely demise.

Creating an effective drainage system is simpler than you might think, and it starts before you even add soil to your container. When selecting a pot, make sure it has one or more drainage holes at the bottom. If not, don't fret—you can easily drill holes yourself using a standard drill and a bit that is suitable for the pot's material. This simple step allows excess water to escape, preventing saturation. Liners, often made of plastic or fabric, can also help manage moisture levels. They act as a barrier between the soil and the container, reducing the risk of waterlogging. Once you've tackled the holes, consider layering the bottom of your pot with gravel or small stones. This technique creates a reservoir for excess water, keeping it away from plant roots. It's a straightforward method that can significantly improve your plant's health.

To further enhance drainage, consider using aids like pot feet or risers. Elevating the pot slightly ensures air can circulate beneath it, promoting better water flow. Drainage mats or mesh are also excellent options. They sit at the bottom of your pot, offering an additional layer that helps water move out efficiently. These products are particularly useful in areas with heavy rainfall or for gardeners who might occasionally overwater. They're like a safety net for your plants, providing extra protection against water-related issues.

Regular maintenance is key to ensuring your drainage system remains effective. Over time, soil and debris can clog drainage holes, so it's wise to check them periodically and clear any blockages. Seasonal changes also affect drainage. During wet months, you might need to elevate your pots more or reduce watering frequency. Conversely, in dry spells, adjust your watering schedule as needed to ensure that your soil doesn't dry out too quickly. These small, attentive practices can make a big difference in maintaining a healthy garden.

Anecdote time: I recall a particularly rainy summer when my lavender started to droop. I realized the drainage setup wasn't coping well with the excess water. Adding a set of pot feet and checking the drainage holes made all the difference. The lavender bounced back, and I learned a valuable lesson in drainage management. These experiences remind us that gardening is as much about observation and adaptation as it is about planning. So, keep an eye on your plants and their containers, and don't hesitate to make adjustments. Your plants will thank you with vibrant growth and lush, healthy foliage.

1.5 ESSENTIAL TOOLS FOR CONTAINER GARDENING: WHAT YOU REALLY NEED

Let's talk tools. Imagine setting out to bake a cake without a measuring cup or a mixing bowl. It would be a challenge, right? The same principle applies to container gardening. Having the right tools can make all the difference between a smooth planting experience and a frustrating one. First on the list is a hand trowel. This small, shovel-like tool is your best friend when it comes to digging, planting, and moving soil around. It's lightweight yet sturdy, perfect for maneuvering in those tight spaces of a container. Next up are pruners. These are used to trim and shape plants, keeping them healthy and encouraging growth. A good pair of pruners should be easy to handle and sharp enough to cut through stems without damaging them.

A watering can is indispensable in your gardening kit. Choose one with a long spout for reaching into pots without disturbing the soil. It's the most efficient way to water your plants evenly and thoroughly. A soil scoop is another handy tool—it's like a bigger version of a spoon, designed to move soil without making a mess. And let's not forget a good pair of gardening gloves. They'll protect your hands from thorns, dirt, and pests, making your gardening experience more comfortable. With these basic tools, you're equipped to tackle most tasks that come your way.

Using your tools properly ensures they last longer and work effectively. Pruners, for instance, should be cleaned after each use to prevent the spread of disease between plants. A quick wipe with a cloth and a dab of oil keeps them rust-free. Sharpening them regularly will make your cuts clean and precise, promoting healthier plant growth. Storing your tools correctly is equally important. Keep them in a dry, sheltered place to avoid rust and wear. A simple pegboard or a toolbox can keep your tools organized and ready for action whenever you need them.

Once you've got the basics, you might feel adventurous and ready to explore advanced techniques. That's where optional tools come in. A moisture meter can be a game-changer. It tells you exactly how wet or dry your soil is, taking the guesswork out of watering. This can prevent overwatering, a common mistake among beginners. Fertilizer spreaders are another great addition. They distribute nutrients evenly, ensuring each plant gets its fair share. Though not essential at the beginning, these tools can enhance your gardening experience as you grow more confident and curious about optimizing plant care.

Gardening tools can be an investment, but there are ways to save without sacrificing quality. Look for multi-purpose tools that can perform several functions, reducing the number of items you need to buy. For instance, some trowels have marked measurements, doubling as a depth guide when planting. Another tip is to browse second-hand stores or online marketplaces for deals. Many gardeners sell their gently used tools at a fraction of the cost. This approach is both budget-friendly and environmentally conscious, as you're giving items a second life.

In the world of gardening, tools are your allies. They make tasks easier, save time, and protect you and your plants. As you gather your collection, remember that quality often trumps quantity. A few well-chosen, well-maintained tools will serve you better than a drawer full of unused gadgets. Start with the basics, take care of them, and gradually build your toolkit as your confidence and skills blossom. With the right tools in hand, you'll find that container gardening becomes not just manageable, but truly enjoyable.

1.6 PLANNING YOUR SPACE: MAPPING OUT YOUR SMALL GARDEN

Picture this: you're standing in your living room, a cup of coffee in hand, gazing out at your tiny balcony or that cozy corner of your yard. This is where your container garden will flourish. But before you start digging into soil and choosing plants, you'll need a plan. Understanding your space is the first step. Measure the area you have available. Is it a narrow balcony or a small patio? Every square foot counts, so get a sense of what you're working with. Light exposure is crucial. Observe how the sun moves across your space throughout the day. Some areas may bask in sunlight while others sit in shade. Microclimates, or small areas with different climates, also play a role. For instance, a spot near a wall might retain heat, while an open area could be cooler. These details influence plant choices and placement.

Now that you have a map of your space, it's time to think about the layout. Start by grouping plants with similar water and light needs. This makes daily care simpler. You don't want to drench a drought-loving succulent just because it's next to a water-loving fern. Creating focal points can transform your garden into a visual delight. Maybe it's a tall plant in the center or a colorful flower arrangement at eye level. Pathways or clear areas allow easy access to your plants and give your garden a structured feel. It's like designing a room—each element should have a purpose and place.

Maximizing your space involves thinking beyond the horizontal plane. Vertical gardening is your secret weapon. Use trellises for climbing plants like beans or peas. Attach shelves to walls for pots of cascading plants. These strategies not only save space but also add layers of interest. On the ground, stagger plants at different heights using stands or steps. This creates depth and makes your garden appear larger. It's an optical illusion that works wonders.

Your garden should reflect your personality. Maybe you love bold colors or prefer a minimalist look. Incorporate decorative elements like colorful pots, whimsical garden gnomes, or elegant lanterns. Themes can guide your plant and décor choices. A Zen garden with bamboo and stones offers tranquility, while a cottage-style garden bursts with wildflowers. Balance aesthetics with practicality. While a beautiful pot is great, ensure it serves the plant's needs, too. The result is a garden that's uniquely yours, a space where you can relax and unwind.

As you lay out your garden, remember that it's a living, breathing space that will change with the seasons. Your plants will grow, bloom, and perhaps need rearranging. Embrace this fluidity. It's part of the joy and discovery of gardening. With a thoughtful plan and a creative touch, your container garden will not only thrive but become a cherished part of your home.

CHAPTER 2:
USING SPACE CREATIVELY

Not all gardens need sprawling lawns or endless plots of land. With a little creativity, even the smallest spaces can bloom into lush, vibrant sanctuaries. This chapter explores a variety of garden types designed to maximize limited areas and turn overlooked spots into thriving green escapes. From walls to windows, balconies to patios, you'll discover how to garden vertically, overhead, and in every nook and cranny.

We'll start with **vertical gardening**, the ultimate space-saver that transforms blank walls and tight corners into eye-catching displays of greenery. Then, we'll take to the skies with **hanging gardens**, perfect for adding cascading plants that free up floor space while drawing the eye upward. For urban dwellers or those with limited outdoor access, **balcony gardens** provide a lush retreat in even the most compact settings. Whether you're looking to grow herbs, flowers, or a mix of both, we'll show you how to design functional and beautiful balcony spaces.

If you're ready to think outside the box (or pot), **DIY upcycled planters** offer budget-friendly and sustainable ways to repurpose everyday items into charming homes for your plants. And for those seeking an indoor-outdoor vibe, **window sill gardens** bring greenery to eye level, offering easy access to herbs and small plants in sunlit spots. Lastly, we'll tackle **patio gardens**, where a mix of containers, climbers, and clever layouts can transform even concrete spaces into lush, inviting havens.

By the end of this chapter, you'll have the tools and inspiration to create stunning gardens in spaces you never thought possible. Get ready to reimagine your surroundings and bring life to every corner of your home!

2.1 VERTICAL GARDENING

Have you ever looked at a blank wall or a narrow alley and wished it could burst into life? That's where vertical gardening comes in—turning those underutilized spaces into thriving green spectacles. Imagine towering columns of lush greenery, like nature's skyscrapers, bringing vibrancy and fresh air into your home. Vertical gardening is all about growing upwards, a perfect fit for urban dwellers or anyone with limited space. It's not just a practical solution; it's a visual feast. By utilizing vertical space, you can create stunning displays that draw the eye and transform your environment. This method is ideal for growing a variety of plants, from cascading flowers to tasty herbs, all without needing a sprawling garden plot.

The benefits of vertical gardening extend beyond saving space. It allows you to experiment with different plant combinations and patterns, adding texture and color to your living area. This upward approach also improves air circulation, keeping your plants healthier and reducing the likelihood of disease. Plus, vertical gardens can act as natural insulators, reducing noise and regulating temperature. When it comes to plant selection, opt for those with shallow root systems and a penchant for trailing. Think succulents, ferns, and vines. They thrive in vertical settings and create a lush, layered look. Herbs like mint and thyme are also excellent choices, providing both beauty and utility.

Creating your vertical garden can be as simple or as elaborate as you like. DIY enthusiasts might start with pallet frames or trellises—these provide sturdy support for climbing plants and can be painted or stained to match your decor. Wall-mounted planters and pocket systems are fantastic options if you want to make a statement. These setups allow you to plant directly into pockets or containers that attach to walls, creating a living tapestry of greenery. You can even use tiered shelves to display pots at varying heights, making it easy to rotate plants and ensure they get the light they need. The design possibilities are endless, limited only by your imagination and available space.

Maintaining a vertical garden requires some thoughtful planning. Watering is crucial, as plants positioned higher may receive less moisture than those below. Consider using a drip watering system to ensure even distribution, or simply water from the top down, letting gravity do the work. Regular pruning is essential to manage growth and encourage fuller, bushier plants. This not only keeps your garden looking neat but also promotes healthy plant development. Keeping an eye out for pests and diseases is also essential, as the dense nature of vertical gardens can sometimes harbor unwanted visitors. Quick intervention and natural remedies are your best defense.

The creative potential of vertical gardens is vast. Why not try a living wall? These vertical gardens are both functional and decorative, serving as a beautiful backdrop in any room. You could create an edible vertical garden, filling it with herbs like basil and rosemary or even small vegetables like cherry tomatoes. This setup provides fresh ingredients for your kitchen and fills your space with delightful aromas. Edible gardens are a great way to combine aesthetics with practicality, offering both visual and culinary rewards.

Whether you're a seasoned green thumb or a complete beginner, vertical gardening offers a unique opportunity to bring nature into your home in an innovative way. It's a chance to experiment, learn, and enjoy the beauty of plants in spaces you might have overlooked. So go ahead, look up, and see the potential in those vertical surfaces waiting to be transformed.

2.2 HANGING GARDENS:
UTILIZING OVERHEAD SPACE

Imagine your living space adorned with plants that cascade like green waterfalls from above. Hanging gardens are your ticket to achieving this enchanting effect. They are perfect for adding visual interest and creating layers in your home or garden without taking up precious floor space. By elevating your plants, you free up the ground and draw the eye upwards, making the entire area feel more expansive and alive. Hanging gardens can transform a bland corner or a bare wall into a vibrant focal point, bringing a touch of nature into even the smallest of spaces.

Choosing the right containers is crucial for a successful hanging garden. Lightweight materials are your best friends here. Consider macramé hangers, which not only support the weight of the plant but also add a bohemian flair to your decor. These hangers are versatile and can be adjusted to fit various pot sizes. Ceiling hooks and brackets are vital for securing your hanging planters. Ensure they are installed in a sturdy spot that is capable of supporting the weight of the plants, soil, and water. If you're renting or unsure about drilling into ceilings, tension rods or over-the-door hooks can offer alternative solutions, providing flexibility and ease of installation.

When selecting plants, look for those that thrive in elevated environments. Trailing plants like ivy and pothos are excellent choices, as they naturally drape downwards, creating a lush, flowing effect. These plants are hardy and can adapt to various light conditions, making them ideal for different spaces in your home. For a splash of color, consider flowering options like fuchsias and petunias. Their vibrant blooms add an eye-catching element to your hanging garden, brightening up any room or outdoor area. These plants require a bit more sunlight, so placement near a window or in a well-lit area is recommended.

Maintaining a hanging garden poses unique challenges, but with a few tips, you'll find it's entirely manageable. Watering is perhaps the most significant hurdle. Elevated plants tend to dry out faster, so you may need to water them more frequently than those on the ground. A watering can with a long spout or a hose attachment designed for hanging baskets can make this task easier. Alternatively, you can take the planters down for a thorough soak and then return them to their hanging spots. Rotating your plants occasionally ensures even growth and prevents them from leaning toward the light source. This simple action encourages uniform development and keeps your hanging garden looking balanced and healthy.

One of the joys of hanging gardens is their versatility. You can experiment with different arrangements, mixing and matching plants to suit your aesthetic. You may want a calming green palette or a lively mix of colors. The choice is yours, and the possibilities are endless. Hanging gardens invite creativity, allowing you to craft a personal sanctuary above the hustle and bustle of daily life. They offer a unique way to engage with nature, turning your home into a living, breathing space.

2.3 BALCONY GARDENS: DESIGNING A LUSH OASIS

Imagine stepping out onto your balcony each morning, greeted by a tapestry of green and vibrant blooms. It's your personal retreat, a place to sip coffee, read a book, or simply soak in the tranquility of nature. Creating a lush oasis on your balcony starts with a bit of planning. Begin by assessing your space. Measure the dimensions carefully, noting features like railings or overhangs that might affect layout choices. Understanding sun exposure is crucial. Spend a day observing how sunlight moves across your balcony. Is there full sun, partial shade, or a mix? This information will guide your plant selection. Wind conditions matter, too. High-up balconies might face strong gusts, so consider windbreaks or choose sturdier plants.

Designing your balcony garden involves making the most of your layout. For those with compact spaces, creating a cozy nook can transform your balcony into a serene escape. Arrange a couple of chairs with a small table surrounded by potted plants. Use plant screens or tall planters to divide spaces, offering privacy without blocking light. If you have a wider balcony, consider zoning different areas. A reading corner with a soft chair and potted lavender for its calming scent, or a dining spot with herbs like basil and mint within arm's reach. Each section can serve a unique purpose, making your balcony versatile and inviting.

Multi-functional furniture and planters can be game-changers in small spaces. Look for bench planters with built-in storage—a perfect spot to store gardening tools or cushions. Convertible tables that double as planters are innovative solutions, maximizing utility without sacrificing style. These pieces are not only practical but also add an element of surprise to your space. Picture a sleek bench that unexpectedly bursts with greenery or a table whose center overflows with colorful blooms. These dual-purpose items help keep your balcony tidy and functional, all while supporting your gardening efforts.

Safety and structural considerations are critical to a thriving balcony garden. Always be mindful of weight limits. Heavy pots can strain the balcony and cause damage. Opt for lightweight containers or distribute weight evenly to prevent stress on the structure. Secure all planters, especially in windy areas, to prevent accidents. Protective trays or mats under pots can safeguard surfaces from water damage and stains, preserving the integrity of your balcony. These steps ensure that your garden remains safe and sustainable, allowing you to enjoy your oasis without worry.

A balcony garden is more than just plants; it's an extension of your home and a reflection of your personality. Choose a color scheme or theme that resonates with you. Perhaps you prefer a Mediterranean vibe with olive trees and terra-cotta pots, or maybe a tropical escape with palms and bold flowers. Add personal touches like fairy lights for evening ambience or a small fountain for soothing sounds. Each element should contribute to a cohesive and inviting environment that brings joy and relaxation. Your balcony is your canvas, ready to be transformed into a lush oasis that delights your senses and nurtures your spirit.

2.4 WINDOW SILL WONDERS: GROWING INDOORS AND OUTDOORS

Have you ever looked at your window sills and thought about the untapped potential they hold? These narrow ledges, often overlooked, are perfect for creating pockets of greenery that bring life and color into your home. Window sills offer a unique advantage for gardening: access to natural light. This makes them an ideal spot for growing plants that thrive on sunlight. Not only do window sills provide the necessary illumination, but they also keep your plants within easy reach, allowing you to care for them effortlessly. This setup is perfect for herbs and small plants that can flourish in limited space, making your kitchen or living room a lively, aromatic space.

When choosing plants for your window sills, go for compact ones that love the sun. Herbs like basil, cilantro, and chives are excellent choices. They grow well in small containers and provide fresh flavors for your cooking. Imagine reaching over to pinc off a few basil leaves for your pasta or cilantro for your salsa. These plants not only look delightful but also serve functional purposes. Small succulents and cacti are other great options. They require minimal care and bring a touch of the desert to your home. Their varied shapes and textures add an interesting visual element, making your window sill a mini botanical garden.

A few strategies can go a long way to maximize the growth of your window sill plants. Plant rotation is key. Turning your pots every week or so ensures that each side of the plant gets equal light exposure, promoting even growth. This simple act prevents your plants from growing lopsided, which can happen when they lean toward the light source. Another trick is to use reflective surfaces. Placing a mirror or foil behind your plants can bounce light back onto them, amplifying the available sunlight. This is especially helpful during shorter winter days when natural light is limited. These small adjustments can make a significant difference in the health and vigor of your plants.

Creating an aesthetically pleasing window sill garden can be a fun endeavor. Could you arrange your plants by height, with taller ones at the back and shorter ones in front, to create a layered effect? This maximizes space and allows each plant to be seen and appreciated. Playing with colors can add vibrancy to your setup. Choose pots in hues that complement your home decor, or go for a mix-and-match approach for a more eclectic look. Adding decorative elements like pebbles, small figurines, or even tiny fairy lights can enhance the charm of your window garden. It's about crafting a scene that's as delightful to look at as it is to smell and touch.

Window sill gardening offers a wonderful opportunity to bring a bit of the outdoors inside, no matter the season. Whether you're nurturing herbs for culinary use or growing succulents for their beauty, these small gardens can transform your living space. They encourage you to engage with nature daily, offering a peaceful, rewarding hobby that fits seamlessly into your lifestyle. The simplicity of caring for a few pots on your window sill means that anyone, regardless of gardening experience, can enjoy the benefits. So, take a fresh look at your window sills and envision their lush possibilities.

2.5 TRANSFORMING PATIOS: FROM CONCRETE TO GREEN

Picture your patio as a blank canvas, waiting to be painted with shades of green and bursts of color. It's more than just a slab of concrete; it's a potential paradise. Start by combining hardscaping with greenery to craft a harmonious space. Use existing structures like railings and walls to support climbing plants, which can soften harsh lines and add vertical interest. Consider adding trellises or lattice panels that double as support and decoration. These provide a backdrop for plants and create an illusion of depth, making the space feel larger and more inviting.

Integrating a variety of plant types can turn your patio into a diverse garden haven—mix shrubs, flowers, and climbing plants to create a tapestry of textures and colors. Shrubs like boxwood or lavender can act as anchors, offering structure and year-round interest. Flowers like geraniums or petunias add seasonal color, while climbing plants such as clematis or jasmine can weave their way up supports, creating a lush overhead canopy. Use containers of varying sizes and heights to play with scale and dimension. Taller pots can elevate trailing plants, while smaller ones can be tucked into corners, maximizing every inch of space.

Think about creating zones within your patio to define different areas and purposes. A seating area with comfortable chairs and a small table, surrounded by fragrant herbs and flowers, might become your morning coffee spot. Use plant screens or trellises to provide privacy from neighbors, turning your patio into a secluded retreat. These screens can also serve as windbreaks, offering protection for more delicate plants. By organizing your space into distinct zones, you can maximize your patio's potential, whether for entertaining guests or enjoying a quiet moment.

Patio gardens are living entities, changing with the seasons. To maintain them year-round, consider the flexibility of portable planters. These allow you to move plants to catch the best sunlight or protect them from harsh weather. In summer, they might soak up the sun; in winter, they could be tucked into a sheltered spot. Incorporating weather-resistant materials is another smart move. Choose containers and furniture made of durable materials like resin or treated wood that can withstand the elements. This ensures that your garden remains vibrant and your setup stays intact through rain, wind, or shine.

A patio garden invites you to get creative and express your style. Perhaps you're drawn to a Mediterranean theme, with terracotta pots and olive trees, or maybe a woodland feel with ferns and moss-covered stones appeals to you. Add personal touches like string lights for evening ambiance or a water feature for soothing sounds. Each element should reflect your taste and enhance the overall vibe. Your patio is not just an outdoor space; it's an extension of your living space. With a bit of imagination, it can become a sanctuary that delights the senses and offers a green escape from the concrete jungle.

2.6 DIY UPCYCLED PLANTERS: BUDGET-FRIENDLY SOLUTIONS

Have you ever considered that the next best planter for your garden might be hiding in plain sight, right within your home? Upcycling is not just a trend—it's a creative and sustainable approach to gardening that makes use of what you already have. Imagine transforming old jars, cans, or even wooden crates into beautiful planters that add a unique touch to your garden. Not only does this save money, but it also helps reduce waste, giving a second life to items that might otherwise end up in the landfill. It's a win-win for both your garden and the planet.

Let's start with a simple project. Those glass jars sitting idly in your kitchen can become charming planters for small herbs or succulents. Clean them thoroughly, drill a few drainage holes in the bottom, and fill them with a good potting mix. Voilà, you have a stylish, transparent planter that lets you watch the roots grow. For a more rustic look, wooden crates and pallets are fantastic options. They can be stacked or hung, creating a tiered garden effect. Line them with landscape fabric to hold the soil, and you have a sturdy planter ready for your favorite flowers or veggies.

Feeling adventurous? Consider transforming old tires into colorful planters. It's easier than you might think. Start by washing the tires to remove any dirt and grime. Then, apply a coat of non-toxic paint in a color that complements your garden theme. Once dry, fill the tires with soil and plant vibrant annuals like marigolds or petunias. These tire planters can be stacked or placed strategically around your garden, adding both height and color. They're durable, weather-resistant, and provide excellent insulation for plants.

Upcycling offers numerous benefits beyond just cost savings. It allows you to personalize your garden with unique designs that reflect your personality. Each upcycled planter tells a story, adding character and creativity to your space. Plus, by reusing materials, you contribute to sustainability efforts, reducing your carbon footprint and encouraging a culture of recycling. It's amazing how a little creativity can turn the ordinary into the extraordinary.

Safety and preparation are key before you start any upcycling project. Proper cleaning of materials is crucial to remove residues or chemicals that could harm your plants. If you're using pallets or wood, check for stamps or labels to ensure they haven't been treated with toxic chemicals. When painting or sealing your planters, opt for non-toxic finishes that are safe for the environment and your plants. This ensures that your DIY planters are beautiful and safe for your garden and the creatures that visit it.

As you explore the world of upcycled gardening, you'll find that the possibilities are endless. With a bit of imagination and a few tools, anything can become a planter. This approach saves you money and infuses your garden with a sense of creativity and sustainability. So next time you think of throwing something away, pause and consider its potential as your next garden masterpiece.

CHAPTER 3:
PLANT SELECTION MADE SIMPLE

Stepping into the world of plant selection can feel a bit overwhelming— like walking into a nursery and being surrounded by endless possibilities. How do you choose the perfect plants for your container garden? Don't worry—this chapter is here to guide you through the green maze, helping you make confident, informed decisions that will transform your space into a thriving, lush oasis.

From shady nooks to sunny balconies, we'll explore the best plants for every lighting condition. Whether you're working with **limited sunlight** or basking in **full sun**, there's a perfect plant for your space. We'll introduce you to resilient shade lovers like ferns and calatheas, as well as sun-seekers such as lavender and geraniums, teaching you how to care for each so they thrive in your containers.

But why stop at just ornamental plants? We'll dive into the joys of growing **edible delights** like basil, mint, and cherry tomatoes. These versatile plants not only enhance your meals but also bring the satisfaction of harvesting straight from your garden. For those looking for low-maintenance options, succulents are a standout choice, offering striking visuals with minimal effort.

Finally, we'll explore how to choose plants that **align with your climate**. Understanding your region's hardiness zone and embracing plants suited to local conditions is key to creating a garden that flourishes year-round. Whether you're dealing with arid heat or coastal humidity, you'll find practical tips to ensure your plants are set up for success.

By the end of this chapter, you'll have a clear understanding of how to select plants that match your space, style, and gardening goals. With the right choices, you'll create a vibrant container garden filled with beauty, utility, and life.

3.1 SHADE-LOVING PLANTS: THRIVING IN LOW LIGHT

Not every space is blessed with abundant sunlight, but that doesn't mean you can't have a vibrant garden. Shade-loving plants are perfect for those areas that bask in dappled light or sit in the shadow of larger structures. These plants have adapted to flourish in low light, making them ideal for indoor spaces, balconies with limited sun, or gardens nestled under tree canopies. Ferns are among the most beloved shade plants, with varieties like the maidenhair and Boston ferns offering delicate, feathery fronds that add a touch of elegance. Their lush green foliage creates a serene atmosphere, perfect for a tranquil corner of your home.

Calatheas are another fantastic choice for shade. Known for their striking foliage, these plants are like living works of art. Their leaves often feature intricate patterns and vibrant color contrasts, adding visual interest to any space. With proper care, calatheas can thrive indoors, bringing a splash of the tropics to your living room or shaded patio. Both ferns and calatheas prefer higher humidity, so they benefit from regular misting or a nearby humidifier. This extra moisture mimics their natural habitat and keeps their leaves lush and healthy.

Consider plants like hostas and begonias when selecting shade-tolerant varieties for your container garden. Hostas are celebrated for their diverse leaf shapes and colors, from deep emerald to variegated patterns. They're hardy and can tolerate various shade conditions, making them a staple for shaded gardens. On the other hand, Begonias are known for their bold, splashy colors and unique leaf textures. They bring a pop of color and excitement to any shaded area, blooming prolifically even with limited sunlight.

Caring for shade plants involves a few specific considerations. These plants generally require less water than their sun-loving counterparts, but they thrive in consistently moist conditions. Be cautious of overwatering, as it can lead to root rot—a common issue in shaded environments where evaporation is slower. A well-draining soil mixture enriched with organic matter can help maintain the proper moisture balance. Shade plants also appreciate a bit of ambient light. Enhance this by placing them near reflective surfaces or using light-colored pots to bounce light back onto the plants.

While gardening in the shade might come with challenges, it also offers unique opportunities to explore a different palette of plants. With the right selection and care, these shaded areas can become some of the most enchanting parts of your garden. So go ahead, embrace the shade, and watch your garden grow in ways you might not have expected.

3.2 SUN-SEEKERS: BEST PLANTS FOR BRIGHT SPACES

If you have a sun-drenched spot, you're in luck. Sun-loving plants are a fantastic choice for those bright areas that soak up rays all day. These plants are like the sunbathers of the plant world, thriving and growing stronger under direct sunlight. They've got some neat tricks up their sleeves to handle the heat. Many sun-loving species have thick, fleshy leaves designed to retain moisture, a clever adaptation that helps them survive when the weather gets scorching. These plants are pretty tough, too, with an inherent drought resistance that lets them withstand periods of dry soil without wilting.

Lavender is a classic example of a sun-loving plant that's both beautiful and practical. Its fragrant blooms add a pop of color and attract pollinators like bees and butterflies. Lavender loves the sun and grows best in well-draining soil, making it perfect for pots on a sunny patio. Geraniums are another top performer. Known for their vibrant, continuous flowering, they bring cheerful hues to any garden space. They thrive in sunny conditions and are relatively low-maintenance, requiring just enough water to keep the soil from drying out completely. Succulents, like aloe vera, also make excellent choices for sunny locations. Aloe vera is not just visually appealing; its gel-filled leaves offer soothing relief for burns and cuts, making it a handy plant to have around.

Caring for sun-loving plants means understanding their specific needs. These plants can dry out quickly during hot weather, so regular watering is key. However, it's important not to overdo it. Allow the top inch of soil to dry out between waterings to prevent root rot. Well-draining soil is crucial for sun plants, as it prevents water from sitting at the roots, which can cause problems. Mixing in some sand or perlite with your potting soil can enhance drainage and mimic these plants' natural environment. This is especially important for potted plants, where water can't escape as easily as it does in the ground.

Sometimes, even sun-loving plants can get too much of a good thing. At the peak of summer, intense sunlight can lead to sunburn on their leaves, characterized by brown, crispy patches. If you notice this happening, consider using a shade cloth during the hottest part of the day to diffuse the sunlight. It's also wise to watch for signs such as wilting or discolored leaves, which indicate your plant is struggling with the temperature. If you spot these signs, try moving the plant to a slightly shadier spot or increase watering to help it recover.

Sun-loving plants are perfect for brightening up those sunny spots around your home. They bring beauty and resilience, transforming a well-lit corner into a vibrant oasis. Whether it's the soothing scent of lavender or the cheerful blooms of geraniums, these plants thrive where others might wilt. With a bit of attention to their watering and soil needs, you'll find that these sun-seekers are not just survivors but stars of the garden.

3.3 EDIBLE DELIGHTS:
GROWING YOUR OWN HERBS AND VEGETABLES

Imagine stepping into your kitchen and picking fresh basil right off the plant, ready to sprinkle onto your homemade pizza. Growing your own herbs and vegetables brings this simple pleasure to life, offering you the freshest produce at your fingertips. Not only does this mean having access to organic ingredients, but it also brings significant cost savings over time. Plus, there's something deeply satisfying about knowing exactly where your food comes from, free from pesticides and grown with love. By cultivating your own edibles, you contribute to a healthier environment, reducing your carbon footprint with fewer trips to the store and less reliance on mass-produced goods.

Chapter 8 dives into this topic, but here are a few headlines. Starting with beginner-friendly herbs and vegetables can make the process smooth and rewarding. Herbs like basil, mint, and rosemary are fantastic for container gardening. They're forgiving, grow quickly, and add flavor to a variety of dishes. Basil loves a sunny spot and regular watering, while mint is a bit of a wild child, thriving almost anywhere with minimal fuss. On the other hand, rosemary prefers things a bit drier, making it perfect for those who might forget a watering or two.

Vegetables like cherry tomatoes and radishes are equally rewarding. Cherry tomatoes bring juicy bursts of flavor, ripening into bright red gems perfect for snacking or salads. They love the sun and benefit from a bit of support as they grow. Radishes, with their peppery crunch, are quick to mature and easy to grow, making them ideal for impatient gardeners. Leafy greens like spinach and lettuce offer continual harvests, providing fresh, crisp leaves for your salads or sandwiches.

Planting and caring for these edibles include a few simple techniques that can make a big difference in your harvest. Did you know certain plants help protect each other? This is called companion planting and it's worth a try. For instance, planting basil near tomatoes can deter pests while enhancing the flavor of the tomatoes. Maintaining a fertilization schedule is also crucial. Most edibles benefit from regular feeding to support their growth, especially during their active growing seasons. Use organic fertilizers to enrich the soil, keeping those nutrients flowing to your plants. A balanced approach ensures your plants get everything they need without any chemical overload.

Troubleshooting in the garden is part of the fun, and it's important to recognize signs of nutrient deficiencies early. Yellowing leaves can indicate a lack of nitrogen, while a purplish hue might signal phosphorus deficiency. Knowing these signs allows you to adjust your fertilization plan accordingly, keeping your plants vibrant and productive. Harvesting at the right time not only maximizes flavor but also encourages regrowth. For herbs, regular pruning or pinching back promotes bushier growth and prevents flowering, which can alter the taste. With leafy greens, picking the outer leaves when they're young and tender keeps the plants producing new growth. For tomatoes, harvesting when they're fully colored and slightly soft ensures the best taste.

Growing your own herbs and vegetables is a journey of discovery and delight. It's about experimenting, tasting, and sometimes learning from mistakes. There's a rhythm to it, a gentle cycle of planting, nurturing, and harvesting that connects you to the seasons and the earth. Whether you're a seasoned cook or a curious novice, having fresh ingredients at your fingertips can transform your culinary adventures, turning everyday meals into something special. So gather your pots and seeds, find a sunny spot, and start growing your edible delights today.

Check out Chapter 8 for a more in-depth look at growing herbs and vegetables.

3.3 SUCCULENT SUCCESS: LOW-MAINTENANCE OPTIONS

If you're looking for plants that require minimal fuss and bring a touch of the exotic to your home, succulents are your go-to choice. These resilient plants are like the superheroes of the plant world, thriving on neglect and adapting to a variety of conditions. Their thick, fleshy leaves are designed to store water, allowing them to survive prolonged periods without a drink. This makes them perfect for busy folks or those new to gardening who might forget to water regularly.

Succulents are incredibly forgiving and can handle the occasional lapse in care, bouncing back with little effort from their owners.

When it comes to picking the right succulents for your containers, you've got plenty of options. Echeverias are a favorite among succulent enthusiasts. Their rosette shapes and wide array of colors—from soft pastels to vibrant greens—make them visually striking. They're compact and fit nicely into small pots, allowing you to easily create stunning arrangements. Haworthias are another excellent choice, known for their compact growth and intricate leaf patterns. They're like little sculptures, adding a decorative touch to any indoor or outdoor space. For those who enjoy trailing plants, Sedum is ideal. Its ability to drape over the edges of containers creates a lush, cascading effect that's both elegant and easy to maintain.

Potting succulents involves a few key steps to ensure they stay healthy and happy. First, choose containers with good drainage. Succulents detest sitting in water, so pots with drainage holes are a must. This prevents water from pooling at the bottom and causing root rot, a common issue with these plants. Next, use a specialized cactus or succulent soil mix. This type of soil is designed to drain quickly, mimicking the arid environments succulents naturally thrive in. It usually contains a blend of sand, perlite, and potting soil, offering the perfect balance of moisture retention and aeration. This setup allows roots to breathe and grow without becoming waterlogged.

Despite their hardy nature, succulents can run into trouble if not cared for properly. Overwatering is the most frequent mistake made by succulent owners. Unlike your typical houseplants, succulents require less water, and letting the soil dry out completely between waterings is crucial. If you notice mushy leaves or a rotten smell, you're likely dealing with root rot. To avoid this, adopt a "less is more" approach to watering. Light is another important factor. While succulents love sunlight, too much direct exposure, especially in hot climates, can cause sunburn on their leaves. Ensuring they receive adequate light without overexposure is vital. Indoors, a bright windowsill is usually perfect; outdoors, providing some afternoon shade can prevent scorching.

In addition to light and water, airflow plays a role in succulent health. Good circulation helps prevent mold and pests, which can thrive in stagnant conditions. If your succulents are indoors, consider placing a fan nearby to keep air moving, especially in humid environments. This simple step can make a significant difference in maintaining healthy plants. With their low-maintenance nature and striking appearance, succulents are an excellent choice for anyone looking to add greenery to their home without the hassle. Their adaptability to various conditions and ability to thrive with minimal care make them a fantastic option for novice and experienced gardeners alike.

3.4 FLOWER POWER: ADDING COLOR TO YOUR CONTAINERS

There's something magical about flowers, isn't there? Their vibrant hues and delicate blooms have a way of transforming any space, lifting our spirits with just a glance. In container gardening, flowers play a crucial role, enhancing the aesthetics and adding a dynamic touch to your garden. They bring a seasonal variety that keeps your garden ever-changing and full of surprises. Imagine stepping out onto your balcony or peeking into your living room to find a cascade of petunias or a burst of marigolds greeting you. These flowers invite color, texture, and life into your space, turning it into a personal paradise. Moreover, flowers attract pollinators like bees and butterflies, which are vital for the ecosystem. Their subtle buzz and flutter add another layer of beauty to your garden, reminding us of the interconnectedness of nature.

When selecting flowering plants for your containers, consider varieties that offer both visual appeal and resilience. Petunias are a popular choice, known for their vivid, cascading blooms that drape elegantly over the sides of pots. They come in an array of colors, from soft pastels to bold reds and purples, allowing you to create a stunning display. Marigolds, with their bright yellows and oranges, are another excellent option. Not only do they add a cheerful pop of color, but they also act as natural pest repellents, making them a practical addition to your garden.

Achieving continuous blooms with flowering plants requires a bit of attention and care, but the results are worth it. One technique to prolong flowering is deadheading, which involves removing spent blooms to encourage new growth. This simple practice prevents the plant from going to seed, allowing it to focus its energy on producing more flowers. Regular fertilization also plays a significant role in maintaining vibrant growth. Use a balanced, water-soluble fertilizer every few weeks to provide essential nutrients that support flowering. This keeps your plants healthy and ensures they have the resources they need to produce those beautiful blooms.

Flowering plants, like all plants, can face challenges. One common issue is pests such as aphids, which can damage flowers and leaves. To manage these naturally, you can introduce beneficial insects like ladybugs, which feed on aphids, keeping their population in check. Alternatively, a gentle spray of soapy water can deter pests without harming your plants. Balancing sunlight and shade is another consideration. While most flowering plants love the sun, too much direct exposure can lead to wilting or sunburn. Placing your containers where they receive morning sun and afternoon shade can help optimize conditions for blooming.

Incorporating flowers into your container garden is like painting with nature's palette. Each bloom adds a splash of color and a hint of fragrance, inviting you to pause and appreciate the beauty around you. With the right selection and a little care, your containers will burst with color, delighting your senses and creating a haven of tranquility and joy.

3.5 CLIMATE CONSIDERATIONS: CHOOSING PLANTS FOR YOUR REGION

Understanding your local climate is one of the most important steps when selecting plants for your container garden. The climate dictates what will thrive and what might struggle. It's here that the concept of plant hardiness zones comes into play. The USDA hardiness zones, for example, categorize regions based on their average minimum temperatures, which helps gardeners determine which plants are most likely to survive the winter in their area. Knowing your zone is like having a cheat sheet for plant selection. It guides you in choosing species that are naturally suited to your local conditions, reducing the risk of planting something destined to fail due to climate mismatch.

When selecting plants, think about the specific challenges and benefits your climate offers. In arid regions where water is scarce, drought-tolerant species are key. These plants have adapted to survive with minimal moisture, often boasting features like waxy leaves or deep root systems to conserve water. Succulents and certain herbs like sage and thyme thrive in such environments, making them excellent choices for dry areas. Conversely, in cooler climates, frost-resistant plants are essential. These species can withstand lower temperatures and occasional frost, preventing them from perishing when the mercury dips. Consider plants like heathers and certain conifers that are naturally equipped to handle cold snaps.

Mulching is a valuable technique for managing temperature and moisture levels in your containers. By adding a layer of organic material like straw or wood chips on top of the soil, you help insulate the roots, keeping them warmer in winter and cooler in summer. Mulch also helps retain moisture, reducing the need for frequent watering. It can suppress weeds, which compete with your plants for nutrients and water. This simple step can make a world of difference, especially in regions where temperature fluctuations are typical.

Consider focusing on regional plant suggestions that align with your local climate to make plant selection even easier. In coastal areas with milder winters and abundant moisture, Mediterranean herbs like rosemary and lavender are fantastic choices. They thrive in well-draining soils and can handle the salty air. In tropical environments, embrace the lushness with tropical plants like hibiscus and bromeliads. These thrive in high humidity and warmth, bringing an exotic flair to your garden. By aligning your plant choices with your regional conditions, you create a garden that's not only beautiful but resilient.

Choosing the right plants for your climate is about working with nature rather than against it. Understanding your hardiness zone, opting for climate-appropriate plants, and utilizing techniques to manage temperature and moisture all contribute to a thriving container garden. Each decision you make, from plant selection to seasonal adjustments, enhances your garden's success and longevity. As you move forward, remember that gardening is an ever-evolving practice, with each season offering new lessons and opportunities for growth. Your container garden will reflect the care and consideration you put into it, rewarding you with beauty and abundance.

CHAPTER 4:
MASTERING WATERING AND MAINTENANCE

Congratulations—you've picked your containers, chosen your plants, and embarked on your container gardening journey. Now comes the heart of it all: caring for your garden so it thrives. This chapter is your ultimate guide to watering and maintenance, transforming what might feel like a chore into a rewarding and intuitive part of your gardening routine.

Watering is where it all begins. Too much, and your plants might drown; too little, and they wither away. It's a delicate balance, but don't worry—we'll break it down for you. From the principles of hydration to handy tools like moisture meters, this chapter will help you fine-tune your approach to watering, giving every plant exactly what it needs.

But watering is just the start. We'll explore practical solutions like **self-watering systems** to simplify care for busy days and delve into **seasonal maintenance** to adapt your gardening habits as the weather changes. You'll also learn about the art of **pruning and deadheading**, which encourages lush, vibrant growth, and the fundamentals of **fertilizing**, so your plants get the nutrients they need to flourish.

Finally, we'll tie it all together with **routine maintenance tips** to keep your garden healthy day in and day out. From daily check-ins to monthly deep dives, you'll gain the confidence to create a thriving, well-maintained garden that rewards you with beauty and abundance.

By the end of this chapter, you'll be equipped not just with techniques but with a deeper understanding of your plants and their needs. This is where your container garden truly comes to life, and with the right care, it will flourish season after season. So grab your watering can, pruning shears, and maybe even a journal—it's time to master the art of gardening care!

4.1 MASTERING WATERING

Have you ever found yourself staring at your plant, watering can in hand, wondering if you're about to do it a favor or a disservice? You're not alone. Watering can be one of the trickiest parts of plant care, yet it's crucial. Water is like the lifeblood of plants, carrying nutrients from the soil up through their roots and into their leaves. That luscious greenery you're aiming for? It relies heavily on getting the watering just right. Too much water, and you risk drowning your plants. Too little, and they wither away. The journey to mastering this balance is what we're diving into.

Overwatering is a common pitfall for many gardeners. You might think you're pampering your plant, but those yellow leaves and mushy roots tell a different story. That's a sign your plant is struggling to breathe because its roots are sitting in waterlogged soil. It's like wearing a raincoat in the shower—just not a pleasant experience. On the flip side, underwatering leaves your plants looking droopy and sad, with dry, brittle soil that's crying out for moisture. Finding that sweet spot can feel like walking a tightrope, but it gets easier once you know what to look for.

Different plants have different water needs, and understanding these is key. Succulents, for instance, are the camels of the plant world. They store water in their thick leaves and can go for weeks without a drink. They thrive on neglect, so it's best to let the soil dry out completely before reaching for the watering can. Meanwhile, tropical plants are like the divas of your garden. They love consistent moisture and humidity, so their soil should be kept damp but not soggy. Using a moisture meter can be a game-changer, providing precise readings of your soil's moisture level and taking the guesswork out of watering. This tool is your ally in ensuring each plant gets just what it needs.

Establishing a watering routine is about consistency and adaptability. In general, watering in the morning is ideal because it allows plants to soak up essential moisture before the sun becomes too intense, minimizing evaporation. Evening watering can lead to wet foliage overnight, increasing the risk of disease. However, your routine should flex with the weather and season. Hot, dry spells might mean more frequent watering, while cooler, wetter periods will require less. Observing your plants and adjusting accordingly is part of the learning process.

Many people fall into the trap of thinking plants need daily watering, but that's not always true. It's a myth that can lead to overwatering. Most plants prefer a cycle of wet and dry soil, which mimics natural conditions. Allowing the top inch of soil to dry out before watering again encourages roots to grow deeper in search of moisture, fostering more robust, healthier plants. This approach conserves water and promotes a more robust root system.

Watering Reflection Exercise
Take a moment to observe your plants. Feel the soil, look at the leaves, and note any changes after watering. This practice enhances your connection with your garden and helps you fine-tune your watering technique.

Arming yourself with this knowledge turns watering from a daunting task into a confident routine. You'll soon find that your plants thrive under your care, rewarding you with vibrant health and beauty.

4.2 SELF-WATERING SYSTEMS: SET IT AND FORGET IT
Imagine a world where you don't have to worry about whether your plants are thirsty, even when you're away for a few days. Enter the self-watering system, a game-changer for busy gardeners and frequent travelers alike. These systems are designed to simplify your watering routine, ensuring your plants consistently receive the moisture they need. At the heart of many self-watering systems is the wick. This

simple yet effective tool gradually delivers water from a reservoir to the plant, using capillary action to keep the soil evenly moist. Think of it as a plant's personal hydration assistant, working quietly in the background.

Setting up a self-watering container might sound technical, but it's pretty straightforward. Start by selecting a container that suits your plant's size and water needs. Larger plants will require bigger reservoirs to maintain adequate moisture levels. Once you've chosen the right container, the assembly begins. Most self-watering pots come with a water reservoir at the base and a wick or similar mechanism that draws water up into the soil. Begin by filling the reservoir and inserting the wick through the designated hole, making sure it reaches into the soil. This setup allows the plant to draw moisture as needed, reducing the need for daily watering. It's like having a reliable backup plan that keeps your plants happy and healthy.

While self-watering systems offer numerous benefits, they aren't without their quirks. One of the biggest perks is the reduced maintenance. You won't need to water your plants as frequently, which is a blessing during busy weeks. This system also helps maintain consistent moisture levels, which is crucial for many plants' health. However, there are some downsides to keep in mind. Over-reliance on the system might lead to complacency, and you could overlook other plant care needs, like feeding or pruning. Additionally, stagnant water in the reservoir can sometimes encourage algae growth, which isn't ideal for your green friends. Regular cleaning of the system can help mitigate this issue.

Like any tool, self-watering systems require a bit of troubleshooting now and then. Clogs in the wicking mechanism can be a common hiccup. If you notice your plant's soil staying dry despite a full reservoir, check for blockages. A simple rinse of the wick or replacing it can often solve the problem. It's also crucial to monitor the water level in the reservoir. Adjusting it based on the plant's needs and environmental conditions ensures optimal performance. During hotter months, you might need to top off the reservoir more frequently, while cooler weather might require less water. Keeping an eye on these factors is critical to maintaining a healthy, thriving plant.

4.3 SEASONAL CARE: ADJUSTING FOR WEATHER CHANGES

As the seasons shift, so do the needs of your plants. Understanding how these changes impact your garden is crucial for keeping your plants healthy and vibrant. During the warmer months, plants bask in the abundant sunlight, soaking up the energy they need to grow and bloom. But as temperatures fluctuate, their growth patterns and needs change. In the heat of summer, plants may require more frequent watering and protection from the sun. Conversely, winter's chill can slow growth, making it vital to adjust your care routine accordingly. This seasonal ebb and flow means that your maintenance practices must adapt to the climate, ensuring that your plants receive the proper care throughout the year.

Adjusting watering and feeding schedules is an integral part of seasonal plant care. During the active growing periods of spring and summer, your plants thrive on consistent moisture and regular feeding. However, as the cooler months approach, it's wise to reduce watering to prevent root rot, a common issue during winter when plants enter dormancy. Less water is needed as growth slows, allowing the soil to dry out more between waterings. Feeding schedules also shift with the seasons. In spring, ramp up the nutrients to support new growth, while in summer, maintain a steady feeding routine. As autumn arrives, gradually decrease feeding to prepare your plants for dormancy, ensuring they have the energy to survive the winter.

Extreme weather poses additional challenges, but you can safeguard your plants from the elements with a few strategies. Heatwaves can be brutal, causing stress and dehydration. During these periods, consider using protective coverings like shade cloths to shield your plants from the harshest sun. These cloths provide enough cover to prevent sunburn while allowing light to reach the leaves. In contrast, frosty conditions demand a different approach. Frost cloths or even old blankets can insulate your plants from the cold, keeping them warm during unexpected cold snaps. Relocating containers to sheltered areas during heavy rain or storms can also prevent waterlogging, ensuring your plants remain protected from the worst of the weather.

Transitioning plants between seasons involves a bit of preparation and care. As you move from summer into autumn, pruning becomes an essential task. Trim back any overgrown foliage and remove dead or diseased material to encourage healthy growth and air circulation. This prepares your plants for dormancy and minimizes the risk of pests and diseases over the winter months. Re-potting is another important consideration. If your plants are root-bound or the soil has become compacted, re-potting can refresh the soil and provide more room for growth. This step is especially beneficial in spring, giving your plants a fresh start as they emerge from their winter rest.

By understanding and adapting to these seasonal changes, you create a nurturing environment for your plants to thrive year-round. Each season brings its own set of challenges and opportunities, but with a bit of planning and flexibility, you can ensure your garden stays lush and healthy, no matter the weather.

4.4 PRUNING AND DEADHEADING: ENCOURAGING NEW GROWTH

Diving into the world of pruning and deadheading might sound like a task for seasoned gardeners, but trust me, it's simpler than it seems and incredibly rewarding. Think of pruning your plants as their regular haircut. Not only does it enhance their appearance, but it's also crucial for nurturing robust, bushy growth and encouraging a vibrant display of blooms. Give your plants this little boost, and watch them thrive beautifully. When you remove those dead branches or overgrown stems, you're essentially telling the plant to focus its energy on new growth rather than maintaining the old. This redirection of energy boosts the plant's health and enhances its appearance.

Pruning is vital for disease prevention. By removing dead or diseased material, you cut off pathways for pests and diseases that could otherwise spread. This simple act can be the difference between a thriving garden and one struggling with infestations. Each plant has its own rules for pruning, so it's essential to tailor your approach. For shaping and controlling size, focus on cutting back to a bud facing the direction you want new growth to appear. This method guides the plant's shape, much like sculpting. Always use sharp, clean tools to avoid tearing the plant tissue, which can cause disease. A good pair of pruners is your best friend here. Remember to cut at a slight angle, allowing water to run off and not collect, which can lead to rot.

Deadheading is simply the removal of spent flowers. This isn't just about keeping your garden looking fresh; it's a crucial step in encouraging more blooms. Pinching or cutting off these faded flowers prevents the plant from putting energy into seed production. Instead, it channels its resources into producing more flowers. Timing is key here. Regularly deadhead throughout the blooming season. Each time you remove a spent bloom, you signal the plant to produce more. It's a simple yet effective way to keep your garden vibrant and colorful.

Here are some pruning and deadheading tips for 10 of the most popular small-space garden plants:

Pothos (Devil's Ivy)
- **How to Prune:** Cut back leggy vines just above a leaf node to encourage fuller, bushier growth.
- **How Often:** Every 2–3 months or when vines become too long or sparse.
- **Time of Year:** Anytime, as Pothos grows year-round.
- **Tips:** Use sharp scissors and propagate cuttings in water or soil to create new plants.

Snake Plant (Sansevieria)
- **How to Prune:** Remove older, yellowing leaves at the base using clean, sharp scissors or pruners.
- **How Often:** Prune as needed when leaves begin to discolor or if the plant becomes overcrowded.
- **Time of Year:** Late spring or early summer during the active growing season.
- **Tips:** Avoid cutting healthy leaves. Divide and repot if the plant outgrows its container.

Spider Plant
- **How to Prune:** Remove spent leaves by cutting them at the base and trim off baby plantlets to prevent overcrowding.
- **How Often:** Every 2–3 months, or as needed to tidy up the plant.
- **Time of Year:** Anytime, but especially in spring or summer when the plant is actively growing.
- **Tips:** Propagate baby plantlets in soil or water to grow new Spider Plants. Pruning helps the parent plant conserve energy and remain healthy.

Tomatoes

- **How to Prune:** Remove suckers (side shoots that grow between the main stem and branches) to focus energy on fruit production.
- **How Often:** Every 1-2 weeks during the growing season.
- **Time of Year:** Late spring to summer.
- **Tips:** Always use clean, sharp pruning shears to avoid spreading disease. Avoid pruning determinate varieties too aggressively, as they produce fruit all at once.

Basil

- **How to Prune:** Pinch off the top leaves just above a leaf pair to encourage bushy growth.
- **How Often:** Weekly during the growing season.
- **Time of Year:** Spring to late summer.
- **Tips:** Never let basil flower unless you're collecting seeds. Pruning regularly also keeps the flavor of the leaves more intense.

Mint

- **How to Prune:** Trim back stems to about 2 inches above the soil.
- **How Often:** Every 3-4 weeks during the growing season.
- **Time of Year:** Spring to early fall.
- **Tips:** Mint grows aggressively; prune frequently to prevent overgrowth. If it flowers, cut it back immediately to maintain the flavor of the leaves.

Rosemary

- **How to Prune:** Cut back 2-3 inches of growth to maintain shape and encourage bushy growth.

- **How Often:** Twice a year—once in spring and again after flowering in summer.
- **Time of Year:** Early spring and late summer.
- **Tips:** Avoid cutting into old, woody growth, as rosemary doesn't regrow well from those areas.

Marigolds
- **How to Deadhead:** Pinch off spent flowers just above the nearest set of leaves.
- **How Often:** Weekly during the blooming season.
- **Time of Year:** Late spring to early fall.
- **Tips:** Regular deadheading encourages continuous blooming. Remove dead or yellowing leaves to keep plants looking tidy.

Zinnias
- **How to Deadhead:** Cut spent blooms just above the nearest leaf node.
- **How Often:** Weekly during the growing season.
- **Time of Year:** Summer to early fall.
- **Tips:** If the plant becomes leggy, cut back stems by a third to encourage fuller growth and more blooms.

Dwarf Sunflowers
- **How to Deadhead:** Remove spent blooms by cutting the flower stalk back to the first set of healthy leaves.
- **How Often:** As soon as blooms fade.
- **Time of Year:** Summer to early fall.
- **Tips:** Deadheading encourages side blooms. Let some flowers go to seed if you want to collect seeds for replanting or feeding birds.

Maintaining your pruning tools is just as important as the pruning itself. Clean and oil your pruners regularly to keep them sharp and rust-free. This extends their lifespan and ensures clean cuts that heal quickly, reducing the risk of disease. A little bit of maintenance goes a long way. It's also wise to wear protective gloves while pruning. They protect your hands from thorns, sap, and blisters, making the process more comfortable. Plus, they add a layer of safety when handling sharp tools.

Pruning and deadheading might seem like extra chores, but they're vital for a thriving garden. They open up your plants to air and light, essential elements for growth. Over time, you'll notice your plants responding with vigor—more blooms, fuller leaves, and a healthier appearance. So grab those pruners with confidence. Your plants will thank you, and you'll gain a deeper connection to your garden through these regular interactions. There's something incredibly satisfying about stepping back and seeing the neat, healthy result of your efforts, knowing you've played a part in your garden's success.

4.5 FERTILIZING FUNDAMENTALS: FEEDING YOUR PLANTS

Imagine your plants as hungry guests at a banquet, eagerly awaiting a nutritious meal to fuel their growth. Just like people, plants need a balanced diet to stay healthy. Fertilizers are the buffet of nutrients, providing the essential macro and micronutrients that plants crave. These nutrients are like building blocks, supporting everything from leaf formation to root development. When plants lack these vital elements, they send out distress signals. Yellowing leaves or stunted growth can often be traced back to nutrient deficiencies. Identifying these signs early allows you to adjust feeding, ensuring your plants remain vibrant and healthy.

Choosing the right fertilizer can feel like navigating a grocery store with endless options. Organic fertilizers often come from natural sources like compost or manure, which are rich in nutrients and beneficial for long-term soil health. They release nutrients slowly, reducing the risk of over-fertilization. However, they might not provide an immediate nutrient boost. On the other hand, synthetic fertilizers offer a quick fix, delivering nutrients directly to plants. They're usually more concentrated, so be cautious when applying them to avoid damaging your plants. Both types have their place, and your choice might depend on personal preference and the specific needs of your garden.

Fertilizers come in various formulations, each with its own pros and cons. Granular fertilizers are easy to apply and often have a slow-release component, providing a steady nutrient supply. Liquid fertilizers act faster, making them ideal when plants need a quick pick-me-up. They're also easier to mix and can be applied directly to the soil or foliage. Slow-release formulations are like time-release vitamins for your plants, slowly breaking down and delivering nutrients over time. This can be particularly useful for those who prefer a more hands-off approach, as it reduces the frequency of applications. Understanding these options helps you tailor your fertilization strategy to meet your plants' needs.

Creating a fertilizing schedule is about finding the right balance. A monthly application might suffice for most plants, providing a consistent nutrient supply without overwhelming them. However, some plants, especially those in active growth stages, might benefit from bi-weekly feedings. Seasonal adjustments are also crucial. When plants grow vigorously in spring and summer, more frequent fertilization is often necessary. As growth slows in autumn, reducing the frequency helps prevent nutrient build-up. Observing your plants and adjusting your schedule ensures they receive the right amount of nourishment throughout the year.

Over-fertilization is like overindulging at a buffet—it might seem harmless at first, but too much can lead to problems. Excess fertilizer can cause nutrient burn, where leaves develop crispy edges or brown spots. To prevent this, particularly with liquid fertilizers, always dilute them to the recommended concentration. This ensures your plants receive nutrients without the risk of burning. Watch for signs of nutrient burn and adjust your applications accordingly. Less is often more when it comes to feeding your plants. By understanding their needs and providing the right nutrients at the right time, you lay the foundation for a thriving, productive garden.

4.6 ROUTINE MAINTENANCE AND JOURNALING

Think of your garden as a living, breathing entity that thrives on attention. Daily maintenance might sound like a lot, but it's really about establishing a rhythm that keeps your plants thriving. Start with the basics—checking soil moisture to see if your plants need a drink. This simple act helps prevent over- and under-watering, two common pitfalls that can easily be avoided. Take a moment to observe your plants closely, looking for any signs of pests or diseases. Catching these early can save you a lot of trouble down the line. Notice a few aphids? A gentle spray of water might be all it takes to dislodge them before they become a problem.

Weekly tasks are your opportunity to nurture growth and maintain the health of your plants. One of those tasks is cleaning leaves. Dust can accumulate, blocking sunlight and hindering photosynthesis, the process plants use to create food. A quick wipe with a damp cloth can make a noticeable difference. Another weekly ritual involves rotating your containers. Just like us, plants benefit from a change of scenery. Rotating them ensures even light exposure, which promotes balanced growth. Plants can sometimes lean towards the light, so this simple act keeps them straight and robust. It's a small task with big benefits, allowing your plants to thrive evenly.

Monthly maintenance is about taking a step back and assessing the bigger picture. This is the time to fertilize based on the specific needs of your plant species. Some might require more nutrients than others, so tailor your approach accordingly. Check your containers for structural integrity. Cracks or wear can lead to leaks and other problems, so addressing these early ensures your garden remains in top shape. This is also an excellent time to give your plants a once-over, checking for any signs of distress that might have been missed during daily or weekly care. A quick inspection can often reveal issues before they become serious.

Many gardeners keep a journal. Keeping a gardening journal is like having a personal assistant for your plants. It helps you track progress, noting growth milestones and any changes you observe. This can be incredibly rewarding, showing you how far your garden has come. Record vital details about your garden's progress, including planting dates, weather patterns, growth milestones, and challenges like pests or diseases. Many gardeners also jot down their observations about soil conditions, watering schedules, pruning dates, and fertilizer applications. Including photos, sketches, or even pressed leaves can make the journal more visual and helpful. Writing in your journal once or twice a week is often enough to capture essential changes and insights while also giving you a reflective moment to connect with your garden's evolution.

Over time, a garden journal becomes an invaluable resource, guiding your efforts from season to season and year to year. Reviewing past entries can help you identify which plants thrived and which struggled, informing decisions about crop rotation, companion planting, or soil amendments. For instance, you might notice that basil planted beside tomatoes flourished or that peas sown too early one spring were stunted by frost. By tracking these details, you build a personalized guide that aligns with your unique growing conditions. As your gardening skills grow, your journal becomes a living record of lessons learned and successes celebrated—a tool that helps you refine your approach and maintenance from year to year.

Routine maintenance might seem daunting at first, but it quickly becomes second nature. These tasks build a strong foundation for your plants, ensuring they have everything they need to grow and flourish. As you settle into this rhythm, your garden will not only survive but thrive, rewarding you with lush greenery and vibrant blooms. As you grow more confident, these routines will pave the way for more advanced gardening adventures, setting the stage for the topics we'll explore next.

CHAPTER 5:

USING SUSTAINABLE AND ECO-FRIENDLY PRACTICES

Imagine peeling vegetables in your kitchen and realizing those scraps could transform into something magical: food for your plants. Or spotting pests in your garden and knowing how to manage them without reaching for chemicals. This chapter is your guide to **sustainable gardening**, where everyday choices—big and small— help nurture not just your plants but the planet, too.

Sustainability in gardening is all about working in harmony with nature. From turning organic waste into rich compost to conserving water with smart irrigation techniques, this chapter will show you how to garden in ways that are environmentally friendly and deeply rewarding. You'll learn how to build a compost system, create natural fertilizers, and adopt practices that reduce waste while enhancing your garden's health.

We'll also dive into **organic pest control**, exploring natural solutions that protect your plants without harming beneficial insects or disrupting the ecosystem. And for those looking to save water, you'll find practical strategies like mulching, rainwater harvesting, and choosing drought-tolerant plants to keep your garden thriving with minimal water use.

Creativity meets sustainability in the section on **upcycling and recycling in the garden**, where we'll show you how to repurpose everyday items into unique and functional gardening tools and décor. Plus, we'll explore the importance of **soil health**, sharing tips for enriching your soil with organic amendments and introducing innovative, soil-less growing techniques like hydroponics.

Finally, we'll take inspiration from around the world with **multicultural gardening techniques**, showcasing time-tested methods like Hugelkultur and companion planting that demonstrate the incredible diversity of sustainable gardening practices.

By the end of this chapter, you'll have the tools and inspiration to make your garden not only beautiful but also a force for good. Whether you're an eco-conscious beginner or an experienced gardener looking to go greener, this chapter will empower you to create a thriving, sustainable garden that nurtures both your plants and the planet.

5.1 COMPOSTING

Composting turns your everyday organic scraps into rich, nutrient-packed compost that feeds your garden. It sounds like magic, and in a way, it is. Think of composting like recycling, but instead of paper and plastic, it turns organic matter like food scraps and yard debris into a valuable fertilizer that enriches soil and promotes plant growth. By composting at home, you reduce the amount of waste sent to landfills and contribute to a healthier environment by cutting down on greenhouse gas emissions. Composting is a win-win for you and the planet, offering a sustainable way to enhance your garden while minimizing your ecological footprint.

Getting started with composting might seem daunting, but it's simpler than you might think. The first step is choosing the right location for your compost bin or pile. Ideally, you want a spot that's easily accessible and has good drainage. If you're working with limited space, a small bin tucked in a balcony corner or a discreet place in the garden works well. Once you've picked your spot, it's time to build your compost pile. The key to successful composting is balancing two types of materials: greens and browns. Greens are nitrogen-rich and include fruit and vegetable scraps, coffee grounds, and fresh grass clippings. Browns are carbon-rich, consisting of dry leaves, untreated wood chips, and shredded paper. By layering these materials, you create a balanced environment that fosters decomposition. Proper aeration and moisture levels are crucial, so remember to turn your pile regularly and keep it as damp as a wrung-out sponge.

When it comes to what you can compost, the list is surprisingly extensive. Kitchen scraps are a great starting point. Think fruit and vegetable peels, eggshells, and coffee grounds. Yard waste like leaves, grass clippings, and small branches also make excellent additions. However, not everything belongs in the compost bin. Avoid meat, dairy, and fatty foods, as these can attract pests and create odors. Likewise, steer clear of herbicide-treated plants, pet waste, and glossy paper, which might not break down properly. By sticking to compostable materials, you ensure a healthy and efficient composting process.

Composting comes with its own set of challenges, but they're easily manageable with a few tips. One common issue is odor, which typically arises from an imbalance in the compost pile. Adding more browns can help neutralize smells by absorbing excess moisture and balancing nitrogen levels. If you notice your compost is decomposing slowly, consider incorporating compost activators like aged manure or commercially available products to speed up the process. These activators introduce beneficial bacteria and enzymes, enhancing decomposition and producing finished compost more quickly.

Composting Reflection Exercise

Set aside a few minutes each week to observe your compost pile. Note any changes in texture, temperature, or odor. Reflect on what might need adjusting, whether it's adding more greens or turning the pile more frequently. This simple exercise helps you stay connected to the process and develop your composting skills.

Composting is a journey that turns waste into a garden treasure. It's about creating a closed-loop system where nothing goes to waste, and everything has a purpose. As you embrace the practice, you'll find it's not just about nurturing your garden but also fostering a deeper connection to the natural cycles of growth and decay. So start small, experiment, and watch as your compost pile transforms into a powerful tool for your garden.

5.2 ORGANIC PEST CONTROL: NATURAL SOLUTIONS FOR COMMON PROBLEMS

When it comes to gardening, pests can be a real buzzkill. But reaching for chemical pesticides isn't the only solution. In fact, going organic has its perks. By avoiding harsh chemicals, you protect beneficial insects like bees and ladybugs, which are crucial for pollination and maintaining a healthy ecosystem. Plus, you're making a choice that's kinder to the environment and your health. Imagine a garden where every creature has its role, and harmony reigns—organic pest control gets you closer to that dream. It's about working with nature, not against it, which is better for your plants and the planet.

So, what are your eco-friendly options? Let's start with companion planting. This is a nifty trick where certain plants are grown together to deter pests naturally. Basil next to tomatoes, for example, can keep aphids away. It's like having a tag-team partner in the garden. Then there's homemade insecticidal soap, an easy DIY remedy. Mix water with a bit of dish soap and spray it on affected plants. This helps control soft-bodied insects like aphids without harming your plants. Ladybugs are also a great ally. These little critters feast on aphids, mites, and other pests. Attract them by planting dill or fennel, or buy them online for a quick garden release. These methods are simple, effective, and safe for your garden environment.

Recognizing which pests are plaguing your plants is the first step. Aphids are small, pear-shaped insects that suck sap from plants, causing leaves to curl or turn yellow. Slugs, on the other hand, leave slimy trails and holes in leaves, especially in damp conditions. Spider mites are tiny and often go unnoticed until you see yellow speckles on leaves, which eventually lead to webbing. Being able to spot these pests early is crucial. The sooner you catch them, the easier it is to manage the problem. Look for signs like chewed leaves, discolored foliage, or a sticky residue on leaves. These clues will help you diagnose the issue and take action quickly.

For prevention and management, regular monitoring is key. Check your plants frequently, especially the undersides of leaves, where pests love to hide. Early intervention can stop an infestation before it starts. Simple barriers like row covers or nets can sometimes keep pests at bay. These physical barriers protect plants while allowing light and water to reach them. It's like putting a protective shield over your garden. Also, consider rotating crops or changing plant locations each season. This disrupts the life cycle of pests and reduces their chances of survival. Keep your garden clean by removing dead leaves and debris that can harbor pests.

Pest Control Cheat Sheet
Create a quick reference sheet with common pests and their natural remedies. Include a column for the pests, the signs of their presence, and effective organic control measures. Keep this handy for quick checks during your gardening routine.

Organic pest control isn't just about eliminating pests; it's about fostering a balanced ecosystem that thrives naturally. By choosing natural methods, you're nurturing a resilient and self-sustaining garden. It's a small change that makes a big difference, ensuring your plants grow healthy and strong without the side effects of chemicals. Embrace these natural solutions and watch your garden flourish with life.

5.3 WATER CONSERVATION TECHNIQUES: SAVING RESOURCES

Water is a precious resource, and conserving it is crucial, especially when droughts loom over many regions. Reducing water usage in gardening not only helps the environment but can also lower your utility bill. Every drop saved is money back in your pocket and one less drop from our precious water reserves. By adopting efficient watering practices, you contribute to a more sustainable world. When water becomes scarce, being mindful of its use helps ensure your garden can thrive without waste, adapting gracefully to environmental challenges.

In container gardening, specific techniques can make a big difference in conserving water. One of the simplest and most effective methods is mulching. Placing a layer of organic material, like straw or bark chips, on top of the soil significantly reduces evaporation. This keeps the soil moist longer, meaning you water less often. Mulching also helps regulate soil temperature, keeping roots cooler in the summer and warmer in the winter, creating a stable environment for your plants. Another great technique is drip irrigation systems, which deliver water directly to roots, minimizing runoff and evaporation. It's like giving your plants a personal water bottle that only they can access. Drip systems can be set on timers, ensuring your plants get just the right amount of water even when you're not around.

Rainwater harvesting is another smart strategy for conserving water. Collecting rainwater in buckets or jars gives your garden a free, sustainable water source. Install an empty container under a downspout and let nature fill it up. This eco-friendly approach takes advantage of what nature provides, making your garden more self-sufficient. Plus, rainwater is naturally soft and free of the chemicals found in tap water, which your plants will appreciate.

Choosing the right plants also plays a vital role in water conservation. Drought-tolerant plants such as succulents are designed to thrive with minimal water. Native plants adapt to local climates and require less maintenance, making them ideal for water-wise gardening. They often have deep root systems that search for water far below the soil surface, allowing them to withstand dry conditions. With their fleshy leaves, succulents store water efficiently and can survive on little moisture.

To optimize your watering habits, consider using soil moisture sensors. These handy tools measure the moisture level in your soil, taking the guesswork out of watering. By knowing exactly when your plants need a drink, you avoid overwatering, which is not only wasteful but can also harm your plants. Timing your watering to the cooler parts of the day, such as early morning or late afternoon, further reduces evaporation and ensures more water reaches the roots. This practice conserves water and helps plants absorb moisture more effectively, keeping them healthy and hydrated.

Incorporating these water conservation techniques into your gardening routine is a step towards a more sustainable and environmentally friendly practice. By being mindful of water usage, you protect this precious resource while maintaining a flourishing garden. Whether through mulching, drip irrigation, rainwater harvesting, or choosing drought-tolerant plants, every action contributes to a greener, more sustainable future.

5.4 UPCYCLING AND RECYCLING IN THE GARDEN: CREATIVE IDEAS

In a world brimming with disposable items, upcycling offers a refreshing twist, turning everyday waste into garden treasures. Imagine taking something as mundane as an old tire and transforming it into a vibrant planter that saves money and reduces waste. It's practical and eco-friendly, offering an inventive way to decorate your garden while conserving resources. Upcycling is more than just a trend—it's a sustainable practice that challenges you to see value in what might otherwise be discarded. By reimagining and repurposing materials, you extend their life cycle, keeping them out of landfills and giving them a new purpose.

Let's explore some creative upcycling projects that breathe life into your garden. Old tires, for example, can be painted in bright colors, stacked creatively, or arranged to form whimsical patterns, becoming unique planters for flowers or herbs. These tire planters add a pop of color and a sense of playfulness to any space. Another simple yet elegant idea involves using glass jars as seed starters. Their transparency lets you watch roots develop, making them perfect for small herbs or seedlings. With a bit of soil and water, they transform windowsills into mini greenhouses. If space is a concern, repurposing pallets into vertical gardens is a fantastic solution. These wooden structures can be hung on walls or fences, creating vertical green spaces ideal for trailing plants or colorful blooms.

The environmental impact of upcycling is significant. By reducing the need for new materials, you're saving money and decreasing demand for natural resources. This conservation effort translates into less energy consumption and fewer greenhouse gas emissions. Each item you upcycle is one less item contributing to landfill waste, making a tangible difference in the fight against pollution. It's about seeing every potential piece of trash as an opportunity to create something beautiful and functional, aligning with a more sustainable lifestyle.

Safety is crucial when working with recycled materials. Start by cleaning and preparing your materials properly. For instance, if you use wooden pallets, check for stamps indicating chemical treatments and sand down rough edges to prevent splinters. When painting or sealing your upcycled projects, opt for non-toxic finishes and paints suitable for outdoor use. These choices protect your plants and the environment, ensuring that your garden remains a safe haven for all its inhabitants.

Upcycling encourages you to think creatively, pushing the boundaries of traditional gardening. It's about embracing a mindset that values sustainability and creativity, prompting you to see potential in the overlooked. By integrating these practices into your gardening routine, you contribute to a greener planet while crafting a garden that's uniquely yours.

5.5 SOIL HEALTH:
ORGANIC AMENDMENTS AND ALTERNATIVES

Healthy soil is the powerhouse behind any thriving container garden. It's more than just dirt—it's a living system that supports plant growth and sustainability. The structure of your soil determines how well it can retain water and drain excess moisture. Good soil allows roots to breathe and access nutrients, which is crucial for plant health. When soil is too compact, it restricts root growth and hampers water movement, leading to unhappy plants. Think of your soil as the foundation of your garden; without a solid base, your plants can struggle to reach their full potential.

Organic amendments are invaluable for boosting soil health. Compost and worm castings are both star players. Compost, rich in nutrients, improves soil structure and enhances its ability to retain moisture. It's like a natural fertilizer that feeds your plants with essential nutrients over time. Worm castings, often called "black gold," are another fantastic additive. They enrich the soil with nutrients and improve its texture, making it crumbly and easy for roots to penetrate. Coconut coir is an excellent option for retaining water without waterlogging your plants. It's a sustainable choice that holds moisture well, providing a buffer against dry spells. By incorporating these additions, you create a thriving environment where plants can flourish.

Creating your own soil mixes at home is both economical and rewarding. Start by balancing three key components: aeration, drainage, and nutrition. A basic recipe might include equal parts of compost, coconut coir, and perlite. Compost provides nutrients, coconut coir helps retain moisture, and perlite ensures good drainage. Adjust the ratios based on your plants' needs and local conditions. If you have access to local resources like pine bark or sand, incorporate them for added benefits. This saves money and supports sustainability by reducing the need for commercially packaged mixes. Homemade mixes give you control over what goes into your soil, ensuring it meets the specific requirements of your garden.

If you're looking for alternatives to traditional soil, consider exploring soil-less gardening techniques. Hydroponics is a fascinating method where plants grow in a nutrient-rich water solution instead of soil. This system provides plants with a constant supply of nutrients, leading to faster growth and higher yields. It's especially useful in urban settings where space is limited. Aquaponics takes it a step further by combining fish farming with hydroponics. Fish waste provides natural fertilizer for the plants, and in turn, the plants help filter the water for the fish. It's a closed-loop system that mimics natural ecosystems and is incredibly efficient. These innovative approaches offer a glimpse into the future of gardening, where sustainability and productivity go hand in hand.

Soil health is the cornerstone of any successful garden. Understanding its importance and how to enhance it will lay the groundwork for a thriving container garden. Whether through organic amendments or soil-less systems, there are countless ways to nurture your plants and ensure they have everything they need to grow strong and healthy. Embrace these methods, and watch as your garden transforms into a vibrant oasis.

CHAPTER 6:
OVERCOMING CHALLENGES AND TROUBLESHOOTING

Gardening is a journey, and like any journey, it's not without its bumps in the road. Whether it's battling pests, struggling with compacted soil, or figuring out why a once-thriving plant now looks sad and wilted, every gardener faces challenges. But here's the good news: these challenges aren't roadblocks—they're opportunities to learn, grow, and become a more confident gardener.

This chapter is your toolkit for tackling the most common obstacles in container gardening. We'll start by helping you **identify and manage garden pests**, those tiny troublemakers that can wreak havoc on your plants. You'll learn how to spot the signs of pest damage, differentiate between harmful pests and helpful allies like ladybugs, and implement organic solutions to keep your garden in balance.

Next, we'll dig into the **soil**—literally. Compacted soil, nutrient deficiencies, and pH imbalances are all common issues, but they're easier to fix than you might think. You'll discover simple techniques to loosen soil, boost its fertility with organic amendments, and create the perfect environment for plant roots to thrive.

We'll also tackle **plant diseases**, offering tips to recognize early warning signs like yellowing leaves or powdery mildew and showing you how to treat them naturally and effectively. From prevention strategies to homemade remedies, you'll feel equipped to keep your plants healthy and resilient.

Weather extremes, like heatwaves and frosts, can be a gardener's worst nightmare, but we've got you covered. Learn how to protect your plants from the elements with practical solutions like shade cloths, frost blankets, and strategic container placement. These tips will help you keep your garden thriving no matter what Mother Nature throws your way.

And what about those moments when a plant looks like it's on its last legs? We'll guide you through **rescuing struggling plants** with quick fixes and long-term strategies to nurse them back to health. You'll also explore how to find a good balance between light, water, and nutrients—a crucial trio for any thriving garden.

By the end of this chapter, you'll feel ready to face any gardening challenge with confidence. Every obstacle is an opportunity to grow—both for your plants and for you as a gardener.

6.1 DEALING WITH PESKY PESTS

Pests: the uninvited guests in your garden party. They're sneaky, sometimes tiny, but they can cause a world of trouble. My first encounter with these little troublemakers was an eye-opener. I noticed my thriving plants suddenly looking sad and wilting, with mysterious holes in their leaves. After a closer inspection, I discovered several tiny culprits—aphids, to be precise—feasting on my plants. At that moment, I realized the importance of knowing your garden pests and how to manage them effectively. This chapter will guide you in identifying these pests, differentiating between the harmful ones and their beneficial counterparts, and exploring ways to manage them without resorting to harsh chemicals.

Identifying garden pests visually is your first line of defense. Aphids, for example, are tiny, sap-sucking insects that often cluster on new growth, leaving behind sticky honeydew that attracts ants and can lead to sooty mold. You might also encounter spider mites, almost invisible to the naked eye, which spin fine webs under leaves, causing a stippled, yellowish appearance. Whiteflies, on the other hand, are small, moth-like insects that flutter up in clouds when disturbed, leaving a trail of sap-sucking damage in their wake. These pests often cause significant damage, characterized by leaf curling, yellowing, and stunted growth. Familiarizing yourself with these signs will help you take action before the damage becomes severe.

While pests are problematic, not all insects in your garden are foes. Some are allies that help keep the ecosystem balanced. Ladybugs, for instance, are voracious eaters of aphids and other soft-bodied pests. Their presence signals a healthy garden balance, as they naturally manage pest populations. Then there are the pollinators—bees and butterflies—who play a vital role in plant reproduction and biodiversity. Recognizing these beneficial insects is crucial. They should be encouraged and protected as they contribute to a thriving garden ecosystem.

For those looking to manage pests organically, there are several effective methods to explore. Neem oil, derived from the seeds of the neem tree, acts as an excellent deterrent for many insects. It disrupts the feeding and reproductive cycles of pests without harming beneficial insects. You can spray it directly on affected plants, ensuring thorough coverage. Diatomaceous earth is another natural solution. Made from fossilized algae, it acts as a physical barrier, deterring pests by damaging their exoskeletons. Dust it lightly over the soil and plants, focusing on areas where pests are prevalent.

Preventing pest infestations involves proactive strategies that create an unfavorable environment for pests while promoting biodiversity. One practical approach is rotating your plants regularly. This simple act disrupts the life cycles of pests and reduces the chances of a single pest population becoming established. Another strategy is companion planting, where certain plants are grown together to benefit each other, which we covered earlier in this book. For instance, planting basil near tomatoes can deter pests while enhancing tomato growth. This method keeps pests at bay and encourages a diverse and resilient garden ecosystem.

By understanding the dynamics between pests and beneficial insects, you can maintain a healthy balance in your garden. Embracing organic management techniques and preventative measures will protect your plants and support a sustainable and thriving garden environment.

6.2 SOLVING SOIL ISSUES: COMPACTION, NUTRITION, AND PH

Have you ever tried to dig into your garden only to find that the soil feels like cement? That's soil compaction—a common challenge in container gardening that can stifle your plants. Imagine trying to grow with your feet bound tightly. Compacted soil restricts growth, making it hard for roots to expand and absorb nutrients and water. This can lead to poor plant health, as the soil also hinders air circulation, essential for healthy roots. When soil is too dense, water can't drain efficiently, which creates a soggy environment that roots dislike. You might notice your plants wilting or not growing as robustly as they should. This isn't a sign of your green thumb failing; it's a cry for help from your plants, asking for a little breathing room.

Improving soil structure in your container garden is easier than you might think. Start by aerating the soil. Consider using a fork or a trowel to gently loosen the soil around your plants. This process creates air pockets and allows roots to breathe and grow more freely.

Another effective method is adding organic matter like compost or well-rotted manure, which improves soil texture. These materials enhance drainage and provide essential nutrients as they break down, supporting your plants' growth. Think of organic matter as a natural conditioner for your soil, keeping it light and fluffy, much like how a good hair conditioner keeps your locks smooth and manageable.

Balanced soil nutrition is crucial for vibrant plant growth. Each nutrient plays a unique role in plant development. Nitrogen is the powerhouse behind leafy growth. If your plants have yellowing leaves, they might be crying out for more nitrogen. Phosphorus, on the other hand, is essential for root development. A lack of phosphorus could be the culprit when you notice stunted plant growth or weak roots. Understanding these signs helps you provide targeted care, ensuring your plants receive the nutrients they need to thrive. Think of it like feeding a balanced diet to your plants, ensuring they have all the vitamins and minerals they need to grow strong and healthy.

Managing soil pH levels is another vital aspect of maintaining a healthy garden. Soil pH affects nutrient availability; most plants prefer a slightly acidic to neutral pH range. Testing your soil's pH is straightforward with a home test kit. These kits provide a simple way to determine whether your soil is too acidic or alkaline. If you find your soil is too acidic, consider adding lime to raise the pH. Lime is a natural amendment that neutralizes acidity, making nutrients more accessible to your plants. If your soil is too alkaline, sulfur-based amendments can help lower the pH, creating an environment where your plants can absorb nutrients more effectively. Adjusting pH levels is like fine-tuning your plants' environment to meet their specific needs, much like adjusting the thermostat for comfort.

Soil Health Reflection

Take a moment to assess your current soil conditions. Note any symptoms you see on your plants and consider testing your soil's pH. Reflect on the balance of nutrients and texture, and jot down any adjustments you might need to make. This reflection can guide your next steps in enhancing your container garden's health.

Soil issues can seem daunting, but with the right approach, they become manageable. By addressing compaction, ensuring balanced nutrition, and managing pH levels, you're setting the stage for a thriving garden. Your plants will reward you with lush growth and vibrant blooms, thriving in the rich, well-tended environment you've created.

6.3 DEALING WITH PLANT DISEASES: PREVENTION AND CURE

Imagine walking out to your garden, expecting to see your plants thriving, only to find white powdery spots on the leaves. This is the calling card of powdery mildew, a common fungal disease that loves to sneak up on gardeners. It's not alone, though. Leaf spot diseases, which leave unsightly brown or black lesions on leaves, are equally notorious for their damaging effects. Both diseases can lead to weakened plants and reduced growth if not addressed promptly. Recognizing these symptoms is your first step in combating plant diseases. Powdery mildew often appears in humid conditions, coating leaves in a white, talc-like substance. Leaf spots, on the other hand, result from various fungi and bacteria, leaving your plants looking like they've been splattered with paint. These visual cues are not just blemishes—they're cries for help from your plants, signaling a need for intervention.

Preventing the spread of disease in your garden involves simple yet effective strategies. Proper spacing between plants is crucial. It ensures adequate airflow, which helps dry out leaves and reduces the likelihood of fungal growth. Think of it as giving your plants personal space to breathe and thrive. Additionally, always sanitize your gardening tools. It's easy to overlook, but using contaminated tools can spread pathogens from plant to plant, much like sharing a fork spreads germs. A quick wipe with rubbing alcohol or a diluted bleach solution can work wonders to keep your tools and plants healthy.

When it comes to treating plant diseases, going organic offers gentle yet effective solutions. A simple baking soda solution can help with fungal issues like powdery mildew. Mix one tablespoon of baking soda with a gallon of water and a splash of dish soap, then spray it on affected plants. This mixture alters the pH on leaf surfaces, creating an environment where fungi struggle to survive. Copper-based sprays are a great option for bacterial infections. They act as a natural fungicide, helping to control disease without harming the plant or surrounding environment. These treatments require regular applications, so consistency is key. Keep an eye on your plants and reapply as needed to keep diseases at bay.

Choosing the right plants can significantly reduce the risk of disease in your garden. Opting for disease-resistant cultivars is a proactive step that pays off in the long run. These varieties are bred to withstand common diseases, giving you a head start in maintaining a healthy garden. Diversifying plant species can also help. A garden with a wide variety of plants is less likely to experience widespread disease outbreaks. It's like not putting all your eggs in one basket. If one plant type succumbs, others can still thrive, keeping your garden vibrant and alive. This diversity enhances your garden's resilience and adds to its visual interest, offering a rich tapestry of colors and textures to enjoy.

Understanding and managing plant diseases is about observation and timely action. You can keep your garden healthy and flourishing by recognizing symptoms early, implementing preventive measures, and choosing the right treatments and plants. Even the most experienced gardeners face plant diseases now and then, but with a bit of knowledge and patience, you can tackle these challenges confidently. Your garden, in turn, will reward you with its beauty and bounty, a testament to your care and dedication.

6.4 WEATHER EXTREMES: PROTECTING YOUR PLANTS

When it comes to container gardening, weather can be both a friend and a foe. While sunny days help your plants thrive, extreme weather conditions can pose significant challenges. Take heatwaves, for instance. They can lead to dehydration and leaf scorch. Imagine your plants sitting under a relentless sun, leaves parched and curling at the edges. This is a common sight during those scorching summer days. The soil in containers heats up quickly, causing water to evaporate faster than you can pour it in. As a result, plants can suffer from stress, wilting, and even permanent damage if left unaddressed. To combat this, providing shade becomes vital. You can use shade cloths or umbrellas to shield your plants from the harshest rays. These simple tools act as a barrier, reducing the amount of direct sunlight and keeping your plants cooler. Another strategy is mulching, which involves spreading a layer of organic material over the soil. This helps retain moisture and maintain a steadier soil temperature, giving your plants a fighting chance against the heat.

On the flip side, cold snaps bring their own set of challenges. Frost can be a silent killer, especially for tender plants not equipped to handle sudden temperature drops. Picture your thriving plants suddenly drooping, their leaves blackened by the icy touch of frost. It's disheartening but not unbeatable. The key is to be prepared. Frost blankets or burlap can be lifesavers here, acting as insulators to trap warmth and protect your plants from the biting cold. On particularly chilly nights, consider moving your containers to sheltered areas, like a garage or a porch, where they'll be out of the frost's reach. This mobility is one of the great advantages of container gardening and can make a significant difference in plant survival.

Adapting to unpredictable weather patterns requires a proactive approach. Weather forecasts become your best friend, offering a preview of what's to come. By keeping an eye on the forecast, you can anticipate sudden changes and take necessary precautions. For instance, if a heatwave is predicted, you might increase your watering schedule or set up shade cloths in advance. Similarly, if a cold snap is on the horizon, you can gather your frost blankets and plan to relocate your plants to safer spots. Temporary structures, such as windbreaks made from lattice or fabric, can also provide protection from harsh winds, which can exacerbate the effects of both heat and cold. These structures create a buffer, reducing wind speed and helping to maintain more stable conditions for your plants.

In the world of gardening, flexibility is key. It's about responding to what nature throws at you, sometimes with little warning. Whether you're battling intense heat or frigid cold, your strategies can make a world of difference. The more you tune into your plants and their needs, the better equipped you'll be to help them weather these extremes. Gardening isn't just about nurturing plants; it's about learning to work with the elements and finding creative solutions to the challenges they present. Weather will always be a factor, but with the right tools and techniques, you can ensure that your container garden remains a vibrant, resilient oasis, no matter what the forecast says.

6.5 RESCUING UNHEALTHY PLANTS: QUICK FIXES AND LONG-TERM SOLUTIONS

We've all been there: standing over a wilted plant, wondering what went wrong. Those droopy leaves, once full of life, now look exhausted. Wilting is often a cry for help, usually signaling water issues. Not enough, and your plant goes thirsty. Too much, and roots drown, unable to breathe. It's a delicate balance. But here's the good news—plants are resilient. They can bounce back with the proper care. Start by checking the soil moisture. If it's bone dry, give your plant a deep drink, ensuring water reaches the roots. If the soil is swampy, it might be time to let it dry out and improve drainage.

Sometimes, plant distress shows up through discoloration. Yellowing leaves can indicate a nutrient deficiency, often a lack of nitrogen. When leaves lose their vibrant green, it's a sign they're missing something vital. This is where a quick intervention can make a difference. Flushing the soil with water helps remove excess salts that can build up and block nutrient absorption. It's like hitting the reset button for your plant. Afterward, a balanced fertilizer can replenish missing nutrients, restoring health and vigor. Pruning damaged or yellowing leaves is another quick fix. It redirects energy to healthier parts of the plant, promoting new growth and preventing further stress.

For long-term plant recovery, think about adjusting your care routine. Plants thrive on consistency. Regularly monitor their progress and tweak your approach based on what you observe. If a plant seems stunted, consider re-potting it with fresh soil. This not only provides a clean slate but also helps invigorate root growth. The new soil offers fresh nutrients and improved structure, allowing roots to expand and breathe. Remember, plants are dynamic. They adapt to changes, but they need you to gently guide them through transitions. It's about nurturing them through gradual improvements, ensuring they regain their strength over time.

One of the best things you can do for your plants is to be proactive. Regular monitoring is crucial. Keep an eye out for early signs of distress, like slight wilting or subtle color changes. A gardening journal can be helpful here. Jot down observations, what works, and what doesn't. This record will become an invaluable resource, helping you learn from past challenges and successes. It's a process of trial and error, but each experience equips you with better insights for the future. Don't be afraid to experiment. Sometimes, a slight change in watering or light exposure can make all the difference.

Ultimately, rescuing unhealthy plants is about patience and persistence. It's easy to feel disheartened when a plant doesn't look its best. But remember, every gardener faces setbacks. It's part of the learning curve. Plants have an incredible capacity to recover, especially when given the right conditions. With careful observation and thoughtful interventions, you can turn things around. Your plants will reward you with renewed growth and vitality, a testament to your care and attention. So take a deep breath, embrace the journey, and enjoy the process of bringing your plants back to life.

6.6 FINDING BALANCE:
LIGHT, WATER, AND NUTRIENT HARMONY

Imagine your plants as a delicate symphony, each element contributing to a harmonious garden. Light, water, and nutrients are the key players, and they need to perform in perfect balance for your plants to thrive. Light is the energy source for photosynthesis, the process through which plants convert sunlight into food. Without enough light, this process falters, and your plants might appear leggy or pale. On the other hand, water is essential for transporting nutrients within the plant. Too much water can drown roots, blocking their ability to absorb what they need, while too little leaves them parched and struggling.

Managing light exposure is all about finding that sweet spot where plants receive the right amount of sunlight. For those with limited natural light, relocating containers can be a game-changer. Moving a pot a few feet can provide better access to sunlight. If natural light is scarce, especially during darker months, supplementing with grow lights can help. These lights mimic the sun's spectrum, providing the energy plants need to photosynthesize effectively. Positioning them at the right distance ensures plants get enough light without the risk of overheating or burning.

Watering practices, too, require a careful touch. Implementing a consistent schedule helps maintain hydration without overwatering. Morning watering is often ideal, allowing plants to drink up before the heat of the day sets in. Self-watering systems, such as wicking pots, offer a convenient solution for maintaining moisture levels. These systems draw water from a reservoir, providing a steady supply that reduces stress on both the plant and the gardener. Observing your plants' needs and adjusting your routine can make all the difference in achieving that perfect balance.

Nutrient management is the final piece of the puzzle. Fertilizers provide essential nutrients that might be missing from the soil. Timing is crucial here; fertilizing during active growth periods, like spring and summer, ensures that plants have the resources they need to flourish. Choosing a balanced fertilizer that includes a mix of nitrogen, phosphorus, and potassium supports comprehensive nutrition. These nutrients play different roles—nitrogen for leafy growth, phosphorus for roots, and potassium for overall health—working together to keep plants healthy.

Incorporating these elements into your gardening routine might seem daunting at first, but with a bit of practice and observation, you can develop a rhythm that suits both you and your plants. Gardening is as much about responding to your plants' cues as following a set schedule. Pay attention to how your plants react to changes in light, water, and nutrients, and adjust accordingly. This attentiveness not only improves plant health but also deepens your connection with them.

As you explore the interplay of light, water, and nutrients, you'll find that gardening is a dance. It's about maintaining balance and harmony, adapting to your plants' needs, and celebrating their growth. This chapter offers a glimpse into the delicate art of nurturing a garden, where each decision impacts the whole. By understanding these elements, you empower yourself to create a thriving, vibrant container garden that reflects your care and dedication.

In the next chapter, we'll delve into seasonal planning and how to keep your garden thriving throughout the year. With the foundation you've built in understanding plant needs, you'll be well-equipped to tackle the changing seasons and keep your garden lush and productive.

CHAPTER 7:
SEASONAL PLANNING

A garden is never static—it's a living, breathing space that evolves with the **seasons**, each bringing its own opportunities and challenges. Whether it's the fresh promise of spring, the vibrant energy of summer, the gentle preparation of autumn, or the cozy retreat of winter, this chapter will guide you through the art of **seasonal planning**. By learning how to adapt to changing conditions, you'll create a thriving, year-round garden that offers beauty and bounty no matter the time of year.

We'll begin with **spring**, the season of renewal. This is the time to prepare your containers, rejuvenate your soil, and select cool-weather crops and early bloomers like peas, pansies, and spinach. You'll learn how to protect your seedlings from unpredictable weather with row covers and how to set the stage for a successful growing season.

When the heat of **summer** arrives, your garden enters its most abundant phase. Managing this growth means staying on top of pruning, supporting tall plants with stakes and cages, and mastering deep-watering techniques to keep your plants hydrated without waste. You'll also discover how to maximize your harvest, tackle common pests like aphids, and protect your plants from powdery mildew.

As **autumn** rolls in, it's time to clean up your garden, plant hardy crops like kale and carrots, and tuck spring bulbs like tulips and daffodils into the soil. You'll explore ways to extend the growing season with cold frames and learn how to transition sensitive plants indoors to protect them from frost. Autumn isn't just a time of endings—it's also the beginning of your next garden cycle.

And when **winter** settles in, the garden doesn't have to stop. Discover the joys of **indoor gardening**, from cultivating herbs like basil and parsley to caring for houseplants that brighten your space. You'll learn how to use grow lights, maintain optimal humidity, and adjust your care routines to suit indoor conditions. Winter is also a great time to plan for the year ahead and experiment with new ideas, ensuring you're ready to hit the ground running when spring returns.

By embracing seasonal planning, you'll not only keep your garden productive but also deepen your connection to nature's rhythms. Each season offers its own rewards and lessons, helping you grow as a gardener. Whether you're tending to tulips in spring, harvesting tomatoes in summer, planting bulbs in autumn, or nurturing houseplants in winter, this chapter will equip you with the tools and knowledge to make every season a gardening success.

7.1 SPRING RENEWAL: PREPPING FOR GROWTH

Spring is like a gentle nudge, waking everything up from winter's slumber. It's when you see the first hints of green poking through the soil, and the air seems to hum with potential. This is the season when gardeners feel the call to action. Imagine the excitement of those first warm days, the scent of earth filling the air, and the promise of new growth all around you. But before you dive headfirst into planting, there's a bit of prep work that will set you up for success. Spring isn't just about new beginnings—it's about making sure your garden is ready to flourish.

Start by assessing and preparing your containers. After a long winter, your pots might show signs of wear—cracks, chips, or even mineral streaks and algae deposits. These need addressing to prevent issues down the line. Examine each container for damage, especially terra-cotta pots, which can crack in cold weather. A little maintenance can go a long way. Scrub them clean with a simple baking soda solution to remove any stubborn stains or remnants from last year's growth. This gives them a fresh start and minimizes the risk of disease transmission to your new plants. Clean containers mean a healthy environment for your seedlings to thrive.

Once your containers are in top shape, turn your attention to the soil. Soil from the previous year can become depleted, losing its vitality and structure. To rejuvenate it, mix in fresh compost and organic amendments. Compost is like a magic potion, rich in nutrients that invigorate tired soil. It boosts fertility and improves the soil's ability to retain moisture. Testing your soil's pH is also a smart move. You'll want to ensure it's within the optimal range for the plants you intend to grow. If you find it's too acidic or too alkaline, don't fret—adjustments can be made with lime or sulfur to balance it out. These steps create a fertile foundation, encouraging robust plant growth.

As you prepare your garden, consider what to plant. Spring is perfect for cool-season vegetables like peas and spinach. These plants relish the mild temperatures and can be some of the first to hit your plate. Early blooming flowers such as pansies and violets add color and cheer, signaling that spring has truly arrived. These flowers are hardy, tolerating the unpredictable weather that early spring sometimes throws our way. By selecting these plants, you're setting up your garden for an early start to the growing season, with produce and blooms to enjoy before summer arrives.

Spring weather can be unpredictable, swinging from warm to chilly without much warning. To protect your plants, especially tender seedlings, consider using row covers. These lightweight fabrics act like a cozy blanket, shielding plants from late frosts and helping to retain warmth. They're easy to use and can be removed during the day to allow for sunlight exposure. Keep a close eye on temperature fluctuations, as these can impact growth. Adjust your care routine accordingly— sometimes a little extra watering or a bit of shelter from the cool breeze can make all the difference. Spring is a season of change, and with a bit of preparation, you can navigate its ups and downs with ease.

Spring Gardening Checklist
- Container Assessment: Check for cracks and clean thoroughly.
- Soil Rejuvenation: Mix in fresh compost and test pH levels.
- Planting Schedule: Focus on cool-season veggies and early flowers.
- Weather Preparedness: Use row covers to protect against frost and monitor temperatures regularly.

Spring is a thrilling start to the gardening year, offering fresh opportunities and lessons. As you dig in, remember that each action you take is a step toward a vibrant garden.

7.2 SUMMER ABUNDANCE: MANAGING GROWTH AND HARVEST

Summer is when everything seems to explode with energy and growth. Plants stretch towards the sun, and your garden turns into a vibrant jungle. It's a sight to behold, but it can quickly become overwhelming if not managed properly. The key to harnessing this summer abundance lies in regular maintenance and care. One of the most effective strategies is pruning. By cutting back overgrown branches, you encourage plants to grow bushier and fuller. This makes them more robust and improves air circulation, reducing the risk of diseases. Use sharp, clean tools to prune, and focus on removing dead or overcrowded stems. Pruning might feel like taking a step back, but it's a leap forward for healthier plants.

Tall plants often need a bit of support to keep them from toppling over. Stakes and cages are your allies here. They help keep plants upright, especially those laden with heavy fruits or blossoms. Imagine your tomato plants, heavy with ripe fruit, standing proud and tall with the help of a simple stake. Use soft ties to secure the stems to the support without bruising them. This small step can prevent damage and ensure your plants continue to thrive throughout the season. It might seem like extra work, but the effort pays off when you see your plants standing tall and healthy.

Summer heat can be brutal, not just for you but for your plants, too. Keeping them hydrated is crucial. The trick is deep watering—ensuring the water reaches the root zones where it's needed most. Shallow watering only wets the surface, leaving roots thirsty. Aim for early morning or late evening watering sessions. This timing minimizes evaporation and gives plants a chance to absorb moisture before the sun's intensity peaks. Watering during the hottest part of the day is a common mistake that can lead to scorched leaves and wasted water. Adjusting your schedule ensures that your garden stays lush and vibrant.

Harvest time is one of summer's greatest rewards. To maximize your yields, keep an eye on your produce. Vegetables and fruits have a peak ripeness when they're at their most delicious and nutritious. For instance, tomatoes should be firm yet give slightly to pressure, and peppers should be brightly colored and glossy. Regular harvesting encourages plants to keep producing. It's like telling your plants, "Hey, there's room for more!" Pick continuously and you'll enjoy a longer harvest season. This practice not only fills your basket but also prevents overripe fruits from attracting pests.

Speaking of pests, summer can bring unwelcome visitors. Powdery mildew is a common disease, appearing as a white powdery substance on leaves. It's unsightly and can weaken your plants. Combat it by ensuring good air circulation and avoiding overhead watering. If it strikes, treat it with a homemade solution of water and baking soda. Aphids, those pesky sap-sucking insects, can also be a problem. Natural repellents like neem oil or insecticidal soap are effective ways to manage them without harsh chemicals. Regularly check your plants for signs of trouble and act quickly to prevent small issues from becoming major headaches. Your garden is a living ecosystem, and a little vigilance goes a long way in keeping it healthy and productive all summer long.

7.3 AUTUMN TRANSITIONS: PREPARING FOR COOLER WEATHER

As the vibrant greens of summer start to fade, autumn arrives with its crisp air and golden hues. This is the time to prepare your garden for the cooler months ahead. It's about tidying up and setting the stage for a healthy return in spring. You can start with a thorough fall cleanup. Removing spent plants and debris from your garden is crucial. Dead plants can harbor diseases and pests, which might linger through winter to trouble you next season. By clearing away these remnants, you create a clean slate. Think of it as a haircut for your garden, trimming away the old to make way for new growth. Once cleared, consider mulching your beds. A layer of mulch acts like a cozy blanket for the soil, protecting roots from the cold and preserving moisture. This simple step can make a big difference in the resilience of your plants through the winter months.

Autumn isn't just about winding down; it's also an opportunity to kickstart the next growing season. Cool-season crops like kale and carrots thrive in the fall. They're hardy and can handle the dropping temperatures. Planting these now means you'll have fresh greens and root veggies to enjoy during the cooler months. It's also the perfect time to think about spring blooms. Planting bulbs such as tulips and daffodils in the fall ensures a colorful garden when spring arrives. These bulbs require a period of cold dormancy to bloom, so getting them in the ground now is key. It might feel odd to plant when everything else is slowing down, but this foresight pays off with a stunning display when winter finally lifts.

As temperatures dip, some plants will need special attention. Transitioning sensitive plants indoors can protect them from frost and extend their growing season. Begin by acclimatizing them gradually to indoor conditions. Move them inside for a few hours each day, increasing the time over a week or two. This helps them adjust to the lower light and humidity indoors. Before you bring them in, check for pests. Inspect leaves and soil thoroughly, treating any infestations with natural remedies. A touch of neem oil can work wonders in keeping pests at bay, safeguarding your indoor environment from critters that might hitch a ride.

To keep your garden productive even as the days shorten, consider using cold frames or cloches. These simple structures trap heat and protect plants from frost, creating a mini-greenhouse effect. They're perfect for extending the growing season for late-season crops like lettuce and spinach. These tools allow you to harvest fresh produce well into the colder months. Another strategy is to select hardy plants that can withstand frosty conditions. Varieties like Brussels sprouts and certain types of cabbages are known for their cold tolerance. They not only survive but often taste better after a frost, as the cold sweetens their flavor. Embracing these methods extends your garden's life and maximizes productivity, even as the world outside begins to chill.

7.4 WINTER WONDERS: INDOOR GARDENING AND CARE

When winter rolls around, it doesn't mean your love for gardening has to hibernate. Instead, it's the perfect time to bring the garden inside. Indoor gardening during the colder months is not just a way to keep your green thumb busy; it's a chance to enjoy the benefits of gardening year-round. Imagine creating a dedicated indoor space where you can nurture plants, breathe in their fresh scents, and benefit from their air-purifying qualities. This cozy green oasis can brighten your home and lift your spirits during the shorter, darker days.

Choosing the right plants is key to successful indoor gardening. Some plants thrive better indoors, especially when winter's chill makes the outdoor environment less hospitable. Herbs like basil and parsley are excellent choices for your kitchen garden. They add flavor to your meals and thrive on a sunny windowsill. Houseplants such as pothos and peace lilies are also great picks. With its trailing vines, Pothos can liven up any corner, while peace lilies add elegance with their glossy leaves and white flowers. These hardy and adaptable plants make them perfect companions for your indoor garden.

Lighting and temperature play crucial roles in maintaining a healthy indoor garden. Natural light can be scarce during winter, so supplementing with grow lights might be necessary. These lights mimic the sun's spectrum, ensuring your plants get the light they need to photosynthesize and grow. Position them about 6 to 12 inches above the plants for optimal results. Another consideration is humidity, especially for tropical plants. Indoor heating can dry out the air, which isn't ideal for plants that thrive in humid conditions. You might find it helpful to use a humidity tray or a small humidifier to maintain the moisture levels your plants prefer. Simple actions like grouping plants or misting them occasionally can also help create a more favorable environment.

Caring for indoor plants also involves adjusting your watering schedule. Indoor environments tend to dry out the soil more slowly than the outdoors, so you may need to water less frequently. It's a good practice to check the soil moisture regularly by sticking your finger an inch deep into the soil. If it feels dry, it's time for a drink. Overwatering is a common pitfall, so ensure your pots have good drainage to prevent water from sitting at the roots. Keep an eye out for pests like spider mites, which can thrive indoors. These tiny pests are sneaky but can be managed with regular inspections and treatments like insecticidal soap if needed.

Indoor gardening during winter is your ticket to keeping the joy of gardening alive, no matter the weather outside. Not only does it keep your home filled with life and color, but it also offers mental and physical benefits. Whether you're growing herbs for the kitchen or nurturing houseplants for their beauty, indoor gardening allows you to enjoy the therapeutic effects of nature all year long.

7.5 YEAR-ROUND HERBS:
CONTINUOUS HARVESTING TECHNIQUES

Growing herbs year-round is like having a fresh pantry at your fingertips. Imagine tossing bright green basil leaves into a salad or snipping a bit of rosemary to roast with potatoes. It's more than just convenience—it's a way to enhance your meals with vibrant flavors and aromas. Fresh herbs are packed with nutrients and antioxidants, offering numerous health benefits. They're also a cost-effective alternative to store-bought options, which can quickly add up. By cultivating your own, you save money and gain the satisfaction of nurturing something from seed to table.

When it comes to choosing herbs for continuous harvest, consider both perennial and annual varieties. Perennial herbs like rosemary and thyme are fantastic choices. These hardy plants return each year, providing a steady supply of leaves. They thrive in well-drained soil and can tolerate some neglect, making them perfect for busy gardeners. On the other hand, fast-growing annuals like cilantro and basil offer quick rewards. They sprout rapidly and can be harvested frequently, keeping your kitchen well-stocked with fresh greens. Their rapid growth cycle means you can enjoy multiple harvests throughout the year, ensuring you never run out of your favorites.

Maintaining consistent growth for your herbs involves a few simple techniques. One effective method is pinching back the growth. By regularly removing the top leaves, you encourage your herbs to become bushy rather than leggy. This provides more leaves for you to use and keeps the plant healthy and robust. Another strategy is rotating your pots. Light exposure can vary throughout the day, and rotating your herbs ensures they receive even sunlight, promoting balanced growth. This simple practice prevents your plants from leaning toward the light and helps them develop evenly.

Harvesting your herbs at the right time maximizes their flavor and ensures a continuous supply. For many herbs, the best time to harvest is in the morning after the dew has dried but before the sun becomes too intense. This is when the essential oils are most concentrated, giving your herbs their strongest flavor. When harvesting, use sharp scissors or pruners to snip just above a leaf node, which encourages new growth. If you find yourself with an abundance, there are several ways to preserve your herbs. Drying them is a classic method. Gather a bunch, tie the stems together, and hang them upside down in a cool, dry place. Once dry, crumble the leaves and store them in airtight containers. Freezing is another excellent option. Chop your herbs and place them in ice cube trays, covering them with water or olive oil before freezing. These cubes can be tossed directly into soups or sauces for a burst of flavor.

If you're ready to be even more creative, consider making herb-infused oils and vinegars. These preserve the essence of your herbs and make wonderful gifts. To create an infused oil, place clean, dry herbs in a bottle and cover them with olive oil. Let it steep for a couple of weeks, then strain out the herbs. The resulting oil will capture the aroma and taste of your garden, ready to drizzle over salads or bread. Vinegars work similarly, offering a tangy twist to your culinary creations. With these methods, your herbs can bring joy and flavor year-round.

7.6 SEASONAL DECOR:
CELEBRATING THE HOLIDAYS WITH PLANTS

As the holidays approach, the desire to transform our homes into cozy, festive retreats grows stronger. While twinkling lights and ornaments are traditional mainstays, incorporating plants into your seasonal decor can add a refreshing, natural touch. Plants bring life and vibrancy to your space, enriching the atmosphere with their colors and textures. They offer versatility, fitting seamlessly into various holiday themes and settings. Opting for natural decor has its perks. It's sustainable, often more affordable, and provides a timeless elegance that synthetic decor sometimes lacks. Plus, the sight of greenery indoors can lift your spirits, providing a sense of calm and serenity amid the holiday hustle.

Selecting the right plants can make a big difference in your holiday decor. Poinsettias are a classic choice for winter celebrations, their bright red and white bracts perfectly capturing the festive spirit. Pair them with holly, known for its spiky leaves and red berries, to create a traditional Christmas vibe. These plants add color and embody the holiday cheer many of us seek during this time. For autumnal gatherings, consider chrysanthemums and pumpkins. Chrysanthemums are available in a range of warm colors, from deep burgundies to bright yellows, making them ideal for fall decor. Pair them with small decorative pumpkins to create a cozy, seasonal display that celebrates the harvest season.

Getting creative with your decor is half the fun. DIY projects let you personalize your space and engage with the season hands-on. Making wreaths from evergreen branches and berries is a timeless craft that results in a beautiful, fragrant decoration for your door or wall. It's a project that can be as simple or as elaborate as you like, and it's an opportunity to use natural materials right from your garden. For your table, consider creating centerpieces with seasonal flowers. Mix and match blooms like poinsettias or chrysanthemums with candles and ornaments for a stunning focal point that draws the eye and enhances your dining experience. These projects are rewarding and provide a chance to get creative with family and friends, turning decorating into a shared activity.

Keeping your decor plants healthy through the season requires a bit of attention. Display plants often have different needs compared to those in the ground. Poinsettias, for example, prefer bright, indirect light and should be watered when the soil feels dry to the touch. Avoid placing them near drafts or heat sources, which can dry them out. Similarly, holly and chrysanthemums need adequate light and regular watering to maintain their vibrancy. For cut flowers and branches, preserving their longevity involves a few simple steps. Change the water in their vases every few days and recut the stems at an angle to help them absorb water more efficiently. Adding a floral preservative to the water can extend their life, keeping your displays fresh and beautiful throughout the celebrations.

Incorporating plants into your holiday decor enhances the visual appeal of your home and brings a touch of nature's tranquility to your festivities. The process of selecting, arranging, and caring for these living decorations offers a moment of mindfulness amid the seasonal bustle. As you explore the possibilities, you'll find that plants have a unique way of complementing the warmth and joy of the holidays, creating an inviting atmosphere for family and guests alike.

CHAPTER 8:

FROM PATIO TO PLATE, YOUR EDIBLE GARDEN

Imagine stepping out onto your patio and picking fresh herbs, vegetables, or fruits just moments before preparing a meal. Container gardening makes this dream accessible, no matter the size of your outdoor space. With a few thoughtfully chosen pots and the right plants, you can transform a balcony, patio, or even a sunny windowsill into a vibrant edible garden. From cherry tomatoes cascading from a hanging basket to a pot brimming with aromatic basil, your garden doesn't just provide food—it adds color, fragrance, and life to your space.

Creating an edible garden is as much about enjoyment as it is about practicality. Start by selecting vegetables and herbs you'll love using in your favorite dishes. Whether it's crisp lettuce for salads, spicy peppers for homemade salsa, or fragrant mint for refreshing teas, planting what you enjoy ensures your garden becomes a delicious extension of your kitchen. Many edible plants thrive in containers, and growing them this way makes it easy to adjust placement to capture the best sunlight or move them indoors when temperatures drop.

With an edible garden, you control how your food is grown, making it a healthier and more sustainable choice. You can avoid pesticides, grow organic varieties, and reduce food waste by harvesting only what you need. Watching your plants thrive is deeply satisfying, but the true reward comes when your homegrown produce makes it to your plate. Each bite becomes a reminder of your efforts, connecting you to the rhythms of nature and the joy of cultivating your own food.

8.1 GETTING STARTED

Starting your container vegetable garden is an exciting journey that begins with a few essential steps to set you up for success. First, **evaluate your space** to determine the amount of sunlight it receives. Most vegetables, like tomatoes and peppers, thrive with 6-8 hours of direct sunlight daily, while leafy greens and herbs can tolerate partial shade. Observe your space throughout the day to identify the sunniest spots and decide where to place your containers. If light is limited, consider compact grow lights as an alternative for ensuring your plants get the energy they need.

Next, focus on choosing the **right containers and soil** for your vegetables. Deep-rooted plants like carrots or tomatoes need larger, deeper pots, while shallow-rooted plants like lettuce can thrive in smaller containers. Ensure your containers have drainage holes to prevent waterlogging, which can damage roots. When it comes to soil, skip garden dirt—it's too dense for containers. Instead, opt for a high-quality potting mix designed for container gardening, enriched with organic matter or compost to provide essential nutrients and retain moisture. Preparing a proper growing medium lays the foundation for healthy plants.

After selecting your containers and soil, it's time to **plan what you'll grow**. Start with vegetables suited to your climate and season, as these will have the best chance of thriving. Beginners might consider easy-to-grow options like cherry tomatoes, lettuce, radishes, or basil, which offer quick rewards and minimal fuss. Decide whether to grow from seeds or seedlings—seeds are cost-effective and rewarding to watch sprout, but seedlings provide a head start if you want faster results. With these basics in place, your garden will be ready to flourish, and you'll be well on your way to enjoying homegrown produce.

8.2 COMPANION PLANTING FOR VEGETABLES AND HERBS: GROWING IN HARMONY

One of the joys of gardening lies in discovering how plants can support one another. Companion planting is a practice rooted in centuries of agricultural wisdom, where certain plants are paired together to mutually enhance their growth, deter pests, or improve flavor. Think of it as matchmaking for your garden—a thoughtful pairing that leads to thriving crops and a balanced ecosystem.

The science behind companion planting is as fascinating as its results. Some plants release chemicals into the soil that benefit their neighbors. Others create physical barriers, like tall corn providing a natural trellis for climbing beans. By combining plants with complementary needs and benefits, you can maximize your container garden's productivity while minimizing issues with pests and diseases.

When planning your companion planting combinations, consider the space and conditions required for each plant. With a bit of forethought, you can create a harmonious garden to maximize the available sunlight in a smaller space. Try a few of these classic pairings:

1. Tomatoes and Basil
- **Why it works**: Basil repels tomato hornworms and whiteflies while enhancing the flavor of tomatoes.
- **Pro tip**: Keep them in a sunny spot and prune basil regularly to encourage bushy growth.
- **Container**: A deep and wide pot, 18–24 inches in diameter and 12–18 inches deep.
- **Why**: Tomatoes need depth for their roots, while basil thrives in the same nutrient-rich soil without taking up much space.

2. Carrots and Chives
- **Why it works**: Chives deter carrot flies, and their shallow roots don't compete with carrots' deep roots.
- **Pro tip**: Plant in loose, sandy soil to allow carrots to grow straight and long.

- **Container**: Opt for a rectangular trough-style container that is at least 12 inches deep and 24 inches long.
- **Reason:** The length accommodates the rows of carrots, while chives' shallow roots fit comfortably along the edges without competing for space.

3. Cucumbers and Nasturtiums
- **Why it works**: Nasturtiums attract aphids and other pests away from cucumbers, acting as a "trap crop."
- **Pro tip**: Nasturtiums also enhance pollination by attracting beneficial insects.
- **Container**: Use a large rectangular or oval container at least 18 inches deep and 24-30 inches wide, with a trellis or cage.
- **Reason**: The depth supports cucumbers' roots, and the wide surface area allows nasturtiums to spread and trail over the sides, doubling as a natural mulch.

4. Peppers and Marigolds
- **Why it works**: Marigolds repel nematodes and aphids, protecting the pepper plants.
- **Pro tip**: Use French marigolds for the best pest control benefits.
- **Container**: A 16-inch-diameter pot that is at least 12-14 inches deep works well for one pepper plant surrounded by marigolds.
- **Reason**: Peppers benefit from deep soil, and the marigolds thrive in the top layer, keeping pests at bay without crowding the peppers.

5. Lettuce and Radishes

- **Why it works**: Radishes grow quickly and loosen the soil, creating space for lettuce roots to spread.
- **Pro tip**: Harvest radishes early to avoid shading the slower-growing lettuce.
- **Container:** Use a shallow, wide container at least 8 inches deep and 18-24 inches wide.
- **Reason:** The shallow depth supports the fast-growing radishes while leaving plenty of space for the lettuce's shallow roots to spread.

6. Spinach and Strawberries

- **Why it works**: Spinach shades the soil, keeping it cool and moist, which strawberries love.
- **Pro tip**: Mulch around the plants to retain moisture and deter slugs.
- **Container**: A tiered or tier-style container with at least 6-8 inches of depth for spinach on the top and 8-10 inches for strawberries at the base.
- **Reason:** The tiered design mimics their natural preference for layered planting, with spinach shading the strawberries while strawberries thrive in the cooler, moister soil below

7. Cabbage and Dill

- **Why it works**: Dill attracts beneficial insects like wasps that prey on cabbage worms, protecting your cabbage.
- **Pro tip**: Avoid planting dill near carrots as it can inhibit their growth.
- **Container:** Use a 20-inch-diameter round container with a depth of 12-16 inches to accommodate the cabbage's large head and dill's feathery stalks.

- **Reason:** Cabbage needs space for its wide head, and dill can grow tall without overshadowing the cabbage, thriving in the same nutrient-rich soil.

8. Zucchini and Borage (Star Flower)
- **Why it works**: Borage deters squash pests like cucumber beetles and enhances pollination with its vibrant flowers.
- **Pro tip**: Borage self-seeds easily, so monitor its spread in your garden.
- **Container:** A large rectangular container that is at least 18 inches deep and 24-30 inches wide works best, with plenty of airflow around the zucchini.
- **Reason:** Zucchini's sprawling vines need room, while borage grows upright, complementing the zucchini's space needs and attracting pollinators.

9. Cabbage and Nasturtiums
- **Why it works**: Nasturtiums act as a trap crop, attracting cabbage moths and aphids away from cabbage.
- **Pro tip**: Plant nasturtiums at the base of cabbage rows to maximize their pest-attracting effect.
- **Container**: A 24-inch diameter round container with a depth of at least 12 inches.
- **Reason:** This size accommodates the cabbage's wide growth and root system while providing space around the edges for trailing nasturtiums to cascade attractively.

10. Zucchini and Beans
- **Why it works**: Beans fix nitrogen in the soil, which zucchini plants use to produce abundant foliage and fruit.

- **Pro tip**: Use bush beans instead of pole beans to avoid overcrowding the zucchini plants.
- **Container:** A 20-inch diameter and 18-inch deep cylindrical pot with a trellis attachment.
- **Reason:** The deep container supports zucchini roots, while the trellis helps bush beans grow vertically, preventing overcrowding.

11. Eggplant and Thyme
- **Why it works**: Thyme repels pests like flea beetles, which commonly attack eggplants.
- **Pro tip**: Allow thyme to bloom—it attracts pollinators that also help eggplants thrive.
- **Container:** A 16-inch-wide and 14-inch-deep terracotta pot.
- **Reason:** The size is perfect for eggplant roots, and terracotta helps regulate moisture for thyme, which prefers drier conditions.

12. Peas and Spinach
- **Why it works**: Peas fix nitrogen into the soil, enriching it for spinach, while spinach grows quickly and can be harvested before the peas need more space.
- **Pro tip**: Succession plant spinach to keep the soil covered even after harvesting.
- **Container**: A long trough-style planter, 12 inches deep and 24 inches wide.
- **Reason:** The length supports rows of peas along one edge with spinach growing low at the base, and it optimizes nitrogen sharing between plants.

13. Carrots and Tomatoes
- **Why it works**: Tomatoes provide partial shade to carrots in hot climates, while carrots aerate the soil for tomato roots.
- **Pro tip**: Ensure good airflow between tomato plants to prevent shading out the carrots completely.
- **Container:** A 24-inch-tall, 18-inch-wide barrel-style pot.
- **Reason:** The tall barrel provides depth for carrot roots to grow straight and ample space for tomato roots and their aerial canopy.

14. Kale and Mint
- **Why it works**: Mint repels cabbage moths, aphids, and flea beetles, protecting kale leaves from damage.
- **Pro tip**: Keep mint in a container near kale to prevent its aggressive spread.
- **Container:** A 16-inch-diameter ceramic or plastic pot with a separate mint pot placed nearby.
- **Reason:** Kale thrives in its own container, while mint's vigorous spreading is contained in its separate pot to prevent overgrowth.

15. Radishes and Cucumbers
1. **Why it works**: Radishes deter cucumber beetles, while their quick growth means they'll be harvested long before cucumbers spread.
2. **Pro tip**: Plant radishes in a ring around your cucumber container to create a natural pest barrier.
3. **Container:** A 16-inch-diameter, 12-inch-deep pot with a built-in trellis.
4. **Reason:** Radishes grow quickly in shallow soil while cucumbers climb the trellis, keeping space usage efficient and preventing pest congregation.

CHAPTER 9:
PERSONALIZATION, COMMUNITY, AND WELL-BEING

Imagine stepping into a garden that feels like an extension of yourself—a space that reflects your personality, nurtures your well-being, and connects you to a larger community. Container gardening offers a unique opportunity to create a **personalized retreat**, no matter the size of your space. Whether you prefer a vibrant, colorful haven or a minimalist sanctuary, this chapter will show you how to design a garden that truly speaks to you.

We'll begin by exploring how to **personalize** your garden. Your choice of plants, colors, and decorative elements can transform your space into a reflection of your style. Picture pots painted in your favorite hues, themes like a tranquil Zen garden or a lively cottage-style oasis, and decorative touches like handmade art, wind chimes, or aromatic plants that delight the senses. Your garden can be as unique as you are, a canvas for self-expression that brings joy and comfort.

Next, we'll dive into the power of **community**. Gardening isn't just a solitary activity—it's a way to **connect with others** who share your passion. From plant swaps to garden tours, engaging with a gardening community lets you share experiences, swap tips, and gain inspiration. Online gardening forums and local clubs offer opportunities to learn and collaborate with gardeners near and far. These connections can turn gardening into a shared journey where you not only grow plants but also build friendships.

Beyond the creative and social aspects, gardening offers profound benefits for your **well-being**. It's a practice that fosters **mindfulness**, helping you focus on the present moment and find relief from stress. Tasks like watering, planting, and pruning become meditative, while the simple act of caring for plants brings a sense of accomplishment and calm. Designing a garden space with soothing features like scented plants, soft lighting, and cozy seating can create a sanctuary where you can relax and recharge.

Whether you're looking to express your creativity, connect with others, or find peace in your daily routine, this chapter will guide you in making your garden a deeply personal and meaningful space. By the end, you'll have the tools and inspiration to create a garden that not only thrives but also enriches your life in unexpected ways

9.1 PERSONALIZATION

When I first started container gardening, I imagined a garden that would reflect my personal style—a space that would make me feel at home and uniquely me. The beauty of container gardening is that it allows for this creative freedom. Whether you're a fan of vibrant hues or prefer a more muted, zen-like environment, your garden can be a true expression of your personality. By choosing colors that resonate with you, your garden becomes a canvas. Imagine pots painted in your favorite shades, perhaps echoing the colors that bring you joy in other aspects of life. Whether it's the calming blues of a coastal retreat or the fiery reds and oranges of a sunset, color can transform your garden into a personal sanctuary.

Incorporating themed designs can further enhance this personal touch. A Zen garden, for example, might feature simple lines and soothing greens with small bamboo plants and smooth stones, creating a space of tranquility and reflection. On the other hand, a cottage garden theme could embrace a riot of colors and textures with wildflowers and rustic wooden containers, inviting a sense of whimsy and charm. Themes allow you to align your gardening space with your interests and tastes, making it a true reflection of who you are.

Decorative elements play a significant role in personalizing your garden. Handmade or custom-painted pots add a personal touch, allowing you to showcase your creativity. These could be pots painted with intricate patterns or simple, bold colors that catch the eye. Garden art, such as sculptures or wind chimes, brings another layer of depth and interest. Imagine a gentle breeze setting off the soft tinkling of a chime, adding a musical element to your garden's ambiance. These accessories are more than mere decorations; they are extensions of your style and taste, transforming your garden into a personal haven.

The plants you choose can also speak volumes about your tastes and values. Heirloom varieties, for instance, carry historical significance and bring a sense of continuity and tradition to your garden. Growing these plants connects you to generations past, each seed holding a story of its own. Culturally significant plants can serve as a nod to your heritage or interests, deepening your connection to your garden. Perhaps you choose to grow a plant that reminds you of a childhood home or a place you've traveled to—these choices infuse your garden with personal meaning and nostalgia.

Creating mood and ambiance in your garden is all about the sensory experience. Scented plants can add an aromatherapy element, turning your garden into a fragrant retreat. Imagine the calming scent of lavender or the refreshing aroma of mint wafting through the air as you sit among your plants. Lighting is another powerful tool for setting the tone. Soft, warm lights can make your garden a cozy, inviting space during the evening. String lights or lanterns can highlight paths or focal points, creating a magical atmosphere that invites relaxation and enjoyment long after the sun has set.

Personalizing your garden is about more than aesthetics. It's about creating a space that feels like an extension of you—a place where you can unwind, reflect, and find joy. Your garden becomes a living, breathing part of your home, filled with elements that inspire and comfort you.

9.2 COMMUNITY BUILDING: SHARING EXPERIENCES AND TIPS

Imagine stepping into a world where your passion for gardening connects you with others who share your love for plants. Engaging with a gardening community can be a transformative experience. It's more than just swapping tips; it's about sharing the highs and lows, the tiny victories when a stubborn seed finally sprouts, and the lessons learned from each challenge. Conversations with fellow gardeners can spark new ideas and inspire you to try things you hadn't considered. You might discover an innovative way to deal with pests or learn about a plant species that becomes your new favorite. This exchange of knowledge creates a rich tapestry of shared experiences that enhances your gardening journey.

Finding the right community is easier than ever, thanks to the digital age. Social media platforms like Facebook and Instagram are bustling with groups and forums dedicated to every gardening niche imaginable. Whether you're into succulents, veggies, or ornamental plants, there's a group for you. These spaces are perfect for asking questions, sharing photos, and getting feedback. You can also attend local gardening clubs or workshops, which offer face-to-face interactions and hands-on learning opportunities. These gatherings often provide a more personal touch, allowing you to connect with gardeners in your area who understand the local climate and soil conditions.

Participating in community events like plant swaps and garden tours can also enrich your gardening experience. Plant swaps are a fantastic way to diversify your garden without spending a dime. You bring in your excess seedlings or cuttings and exchange them for something new. It's a simple yet effective way to expand your collection and meet fellow plant enthusiasts. Hosting or attending garden tours lets you showcase your garden's progress and get inspired by others. These tours are an excellent opportunity to see different gardening styles and gain insights that you can apply to your space.

Communities also play a crucial role in promoting sustainable gardening practices. By working together, gardeners can create shared composting initiatives, reducing waste and enriching the soil with homemade compost. These initiatives benefit individual gardens and contribute to a healthier environment overall. Community gardens are another excellent example of collective efforts. They provide a space for people to grow their food, reducing the carbon footprint associated with transporting produce. Participating in these gardens fosters a sense of camaraderie and shared responsibility, making gardening a communal activity that brings people together.

9.3 MINDFULNESS IN GARDENING: STRESS RELIEF AND RELAXATION

When I think about the connection between gardening and mindfulness, I see it as a blend of art and therapy. There's something deeply soothing about being among plants, feeling the earth in your hands, and watching life unfold. Gardening has this wonderful way of drawing you into the present moment, helping you forget the chaos and stress of daily life. The repetitive tasks—like planting seeds, watering, and pruning—act as a form of meditation, calming the mind and reducing stress. These simple activities have a rhythm that allows you to focus solely on what you're doing, giving your mind a much-needed break from worries. The repetitive nature of these tasks can be incredibly grounding, offering a sense of peace and relaxation that is hard to find elsewhere.

Incorporating mindfulness into your gardening routine doesn't require any special skills or tools. It's about being present and intentional with each action. Start by practicing deep breathing as you work with your plants. Take slow, deliberate breaths as you dig, plant, or water. Feel the textures, notice the scents, and listen to the sounds around you. Let these sensory experiences anchor you in the moment. Gardening can be a form of meditation, where each step and gesture is made with awareness. This approach enhances your gardening experience and fosters a deeper connection with your environment, promoting mental clarity and emotional balance.

The therapeutic aspects of gardening extend beyond mindfulness. It's a chance to connect with nature, which in itself is a powerful form of therapy. Being surrounded by living things reminds us of the beauty and complexity of life. Plants grow, change, and adapt over time, and nurturing them can provide a profound sense of accomplishment. Watching a seed sprout or a flower bloom is a tangible result of your care and effort. This sense of achievement boosts your mood and builds confidence, reinforcing the idea that your actions have a positive impact. It's an experience that can uplift and empower, especially during challenging times.

Creating a tranquil gardening space enhances these benefits. Designing your garden to be a place of peace and reflection can significantly boost its calming effects. Consider incorporating water features, like a small fountain or birdbath, to add soothing sounds that enhance the sense of serenity. The gentle trickle of water can mask background noise, creating a more immersive, peaceful environment. Designing quiet corners with comfortable seating provides a space for rest and reflection. Imagine a cozy nook where you can sit with a book or simply enjoy the view. Surrounding yourself with calming plants, such as lavender or chamomile, can also contribute to the overall sense of relaxation, thanks to their soothing scents and soft colors.

Gardening is an opportunity to practice mindfulness, bringing together the physical and the spiritual in a way that nurtures plants and people alike. It reminds us that growth isn't just for the garden; it's for us, too. As you tend to your plants, you also tend to your mind and heart, cultivating a sense of peace and well-being that extends beyond the garden gates.

9.4 THE JOY OF GARDENING: EMBRACING THE JOURNEY

Gardening is a unique pleasure that brings immense joy as you witness the transformation and growth of your plants. Imagine the thrill of spotting the first green sprout breaking through the soil or watching a bud slowly unfurl into a vibrant bloom. These moments are small victories, yet they fill you with a sense of accomplishment and wonder. The satisfaction extends to harvesting your own produce, too. Picking a ripe tomato or snipping fresh basil for dinner brings a special kind of happiness that only comes from nurturing something from seed to table. It's a simple joy, but one that deeply connects you to the natural world and to yourself.

Instead of striving for perfection in your garden, please focus on the process and the learning that comes with it. Gardens are wonderfully imperfect, and that's part of their charm. Leaves may yellow and pests might nibble, but each challenge offers a chance to learn and improve. Embrace these imperfections; they are the stepping stones to your gardening education. Find joy in everyday tasks, like watering or weeding, which can be meditative and calming. Each task you perform, no matter how small, contributes to the well-being of your garden, and that is something to celebrate.

Gardening offers more than just beautiful plants; it nurtures personal growth and development. It teaches patience as you wait for seeds to sprout and perseverance when faced with setbacks like unexpected weather or pests. These challenges build resilience and problem-solving skills. You learn to adapt, to try new strategies, and sometimes to accept when things don't go as planned. Creativity flourishes in the garden, too, as you experiment with plant arrangements, colors, and spaces. This creative process enhances your ability to think outside the box and develop solutions to everyday problems.

Lifelong enjoyment of gardening comes from a willingness to explore and grow as a gardener continually. Set new goals, like trying to grow a new plant species or designing a new container arrangement. These goals keep your gardening experience fresh and exciting. Sharing the joy of gardening with family and friends can also enhance your experience. Invite loved ones to join you in planting or harvesting, or share your garden's bounty with them. This shared experience strengthens bonds and spreads the happiness that gardening brings.

Gardening is a journey filled with learning, growth, and joy. It encourages you to engage with nature, explore your creativity, and develop resilience. These experiences are not just about the plants you grow but about the gardener you become in the process. As you continue to explore the world of gardening, embrace the joys and challenges it brings, knowing that each step enriches your life and connects you more deeply to the world around you.

LIFE LONG ADVENTURE

What a journey we've been on together! From picking the perfect pot to mastering the art of watering, you've explored the incredible world of container gardening. The main goal was to make gardening accessible for you as a beginner, breaking down complex concepts into simple, digestible steps. I hope you feel empowered and ready to transform your small spaces into lush, vibrant gardens.

Let's revisit some key takeaways. First, container gardening is versatile, allowing you to grow a wide range of plants, whether fresh herbs for your kitchen or vibrant flowers for your balcony. You've learned about choosing the proper containers, understanding plant needs, and creating the perfect environment with soil and drainage. Remember, it's all about creating a mini ecosystem that suits your style and space.

I encourage you to take what you've learned and dive in. Whether you're starting with a single potted plant on a windowsill or planning a complete balcony makeover, the important thing is to get your hands dirty. Experiment with different plants and techniques. Don't be afraid to make mistakes—they're just stepping stones to becoming a more confident gardener. Share your experiences with friends, family, or even strangers online. You might inspire someone else to start their gardening journey!

Gardening is a lifelong adventure, and there's always more to explore. Set new goals and try growing a plant you've never considered before. Challenge yourself with vertical gardening or delve into upcycling projects. The more you learn, the more rewarding your garden will become. Plus, it keeps your mind sharp and your heart engaged in continuous growth.

Beyond the soil and seeds, remember the holistic benefits of gardening. It's not just about the plants; it's about nurturing your well-being. The act of gardening can be a calming, meditative practice that relieves stress and boosts your mood. So, take a deep breath, feel the earth between your fingers, and let the garden work its magic on your spirit.

I also encourage you to connect with the wider gardening community. Join local clubs or online forums where you can swap tips and stories. Share your successes and learn from others. There's a vast network of gardeners out there ready to welcome you, offering support and camaraderie every step of the way.

Thank you for allowing me to be part of your gardening journey. Your trust in this book means the world to me. It's been a joy to guide you through the basics and beyond. Remember, you have everything you need to succeed. With patience, curiosity, and a sprinkle of creativity, your garden will thrive.

In closing, embrace the joy and fulfillment that gardening brings. Whether you're watching a seed sprout or harvesting your own vegetables, each moment is a testament to your effort and care. Let your garden grow not only in size, but in the happiness and satisfaction it brings to your life. Keep your curiosity alive and your hands in the soil, and your garden will continue to be a source of wonder and delight.

Happy gardening!

REFERENCES

Iowa State University Extension and Outreach. (2020, May 28). *Container gardening: Big benefits in small spaces.* Spend Smart. Eat Smart. https://spendsmart.extension.iastate.edu/spendsmart/2020/05/28/container-gardening-big-benefits-in-small-spaces/

Epic Gardening. (n.d.). *What plant containers are best for container gardens?* https://www.epicgardening.com/plant-containers/

Southern Living. (n.d.). *8 container gardening mistakes to avoid.* https://www.southernliving.com/container-gardening-mistakes

Treehugger. (2023, April 25). *Expert tips for a sustainable container garden.* https://www.treehugger.com/expert-tips-sustainable-container-garden-7549718

Southview Design. (2023, March 15). *Vertical gardening guide | Minnesota.* https://southviewdesign.com/blog/vertical-gardening-guide

The Spruce. (2023, May 10). *28 unique DIY vertical garden ideas to try.* https://www.thespruce.com/diy-vertical-garden-ideas-7481062

Garden Design. (2023, June 5). *21 balcony garden ideas for beginners in small spaces.* https://www.gardendesign.com/small/balcony-garden.html

HGTV. (n.d.). *35+ upcycled container gardens and yard art.* https://www.hgtv.com/outdoors/flowers-and-plants/upcycled-and-whimsical-container-gardens-and-planters-pictures

Garden Design. (2023, July 20). *Best shade plants for pots & shade container ideas.* https://www.gardendesign.com/containers/shade.html

The Spruce. (2023, August 15). *28 best small full-sun perennials.* https://www.thespruce.com/perennials-that-thrive-in-full-sun

Millcreek Gardens. (n.d.). *The best herbs and vegetables for container gardens.* https://millcreekgardens.com/herbs-and-vegetables-for-container-gardens/

Gardening Know How. (2024, April 4). *New USDA plant hardiness zone map: What changed?* https://www.gardeningknowhow.com/garden-how-to/gardening-by-zone/2023-usda-plant-hardiness-zone-map

Fine Gardening. (n.d.). *How to properly care for a garden container.* https://www.finegardening.com/article/container

Lowe's. (2023, January 13). *How to water house plants while you're away.* https://www.lowes.com/n/how-to/water-plants-while-away

Planters Place. (n.d.). *How to prune container plants.*
https://plantersplace.com/pp-featured/how-to-prune-container-plants/

Kellogg Garden. (n.d.). *Container gardening: Swapping for the season.*
https://kellogggarden.com/blog/gardening/container-gardening/
container-gardening-swapping-for-the-season/

U.S. Environmental Protection Agency. (n.d.). *Composting at home.*
https://www.epa.gov/recycle/composting-home

Black Girls Gardening in Containers. (2023, February 10). *6 ways to
control common container garden pests.*
https://www.blackgirlsgardeningincontainers.com/post/6-ways-to-
control-common-container-garden-pests

Grow NYC. (n.d.). *Water conservation techniques for urban gardens.*
https://www.grownyc.org/files/citylot/Water_Conservation_
Techniques.pdf

Sustain My Craft Habit. (2022, March 23). *45 upcycling ideas for
the garden.*
https://sustainmycrafthabit.com/diy-upcycling-projects-for-the-
garden/

Made in United States
Orlando, FL
17 June 2025

62182913R00080